Harveys Kiddermins

C000204579

By
Nigel Gilbert

In memory of my mother, Dorothy Gilbert,
who died 16th September 2010 while I was completing this book

All artwork, illustrations and preparation of photographs by David Gilbert

Hencroft Press 2010
ISBN 978 0 9535442 3 3
© Nigel Gilbert

Printed by: Rotary Printers (Stourport-on-Severn) Ltd., Mitton Street, Stourport-on-Severn. DY13 9AA. Tel: 01299 823839 and 01299 827797

Contents

Acknowledgments

This book has been made possible by the assistance of many people, but in particular I must first mention William Smith and his colleagues at Bristol Record Office. Two boxes of documents relating to Harveys of Kidderminster were found by William in storage, and they have provided the basis for the story. Special thanks are due to Mary Lawson, who worked for Harveys as a very young woman from around 1958 and has given me a lot of encouragement as well as the benefit of her first-hand observations. Archaeologists from Worcestershire County Council have helped me to analyse the photographic record of the cellars, and thanks are due to Victoria Bryant, Hal Dalwood and especially Shona Robson-Glyde. Heather Flack has been exceedingly helpful concerning Edward Prichard and his family. Knowing her interest in Wribbenhall, where he died, I made a polite enquiry about whether she knew anything, and thereafter I could not stop her doing research.

Gill Onslow has enthusiastically assisted with tracking down the detail of some of the family history required, and in particular traced the background of Lydia Harvey. I am grateful to Charles Purcell for enabling me to locate the Prichard grave in Dowles churchyard. Scott Pettitt also assisted with graves, showing me that of James Harvey at St Johns and that of Charles and Lydia Harvey at the cemetery. Melvyn Thompson has helped me to clarify the connections of the Harvey and Jotham families to St George's church. I have had many conversations with John Combe over the years about the Harveys, and his love of sherry has helped inspire this book. I have benefited also from various conversations with Don Gilbert about related aspects of Kidderminster's history. Bob Millward drew my attention to the references to Harveys vault in the diary of George Roberts. Sarah Houle gave me the opportunity to visit Ismere House, where Charles and Lydia Harvey lived, and to study documents relating to the house.

In the period 2006 to 2008 the Historic Kidderminster Project was kindly given access to the deeds held by Wyre Forest District Council. These included documents for the Clarence Inn and 3 to 7 Coventry Street which have been used for this book. I thank staff in the legal department for their help, especially Sue Crowther. I am grateful to the Carpet Museum Archive for use of their hard copies of back-numbers of the *Shuttle*. Thanks are due also to staff at Kidderminster Library, Bristol Central Library, Worcester Record Office and Liverpool Maritime Museum.

Dave Brown made an immensely valuable contribution by photographing the photographs held at Bristol Record Office. I shall never forget the contortions necessary to overcome the awkward lighting conditions.

Others who have helped in various ways include Wayne Bell, Norman and Olive Broadfield, John Fudge, Robert Hart, John Harvey V, Allan and Pat Leek, Trevor Warder, Shirley Williams, and Robin Wodehouse. Finally, I must thank my wife, Ingra, who has been very supportive and who has removed many errors from the text.

Introduction

Kidderminster has been so much destroyed by modern development that it probably needs its history more than does Bristol. So this book tells the story of the famous wine merchants from the perspective of its Midlands base. As it happened, the name of the Kidderminster business carried the Harvey name over a decade before it did so in the family's home city. The story has added spice for Kidderminster people. Their town's legendary cellar, which was thought for centuries to have been an ancient chapel and was so wantonly bulldozed in the developments of the late 1960s, was occupied in the end by Harveys.

The Kidderminster connection of the company, which is renowned for its Bristol Cream sherry, is now largely unknown. In fact, in the early nineteenth century this part of the business was apparently so attractive that it was long told, in Kidderminster at least, that the two Harvey brothers, John and Charles, competed for the privilege of coming to the Worcestershire town rather than stay in Bristol. The truth of this must be doubted. Kidderminster, especially in the decades which followed a great strike of carpet weavers in 1828, was not regarded as a town likely to attract those who would otherwise have resided in the elegant Bristol suburb of Clifton. Yet it is certainly true that for over one hundred years a succession of members of the Harvey family came to Kidderminster to run the business.

The importance of the town to the wine merchants of Bristol lay in its location close to the upper reaches of the navigable part of the Severn. Kidderminster's importance to the river trade has probably been underestimated relative to the neighbouring town of Bewdley. It was a distribution centre, located at a significant road junction, and its cellars offered merchants secure storage prior to moving goods on to the Midlands and further north. The opening of the canal in 1771 enhanced the town's strategic importance. After many decades, of course, communication improved by rail and road, and Harveys' Kidderminster business, which was at first independent but eventually became a subsidiary of Bristol, was of uncertain benefit to its parent company. The international success of the Bristol Cream brand, coupled with the remorseless capitalist drive for ever greater profits, made the old Kidderminster premises with its cellars increasingly irrelevant. The narrative really ends at the end of 1967 with their closure. However, as a postscript it has to be noted that continued expansion and globalisation has since seen Harveys removed from Bristol as well.

The basis of the book is a series of chapters telling the story of the business as it happened from the late eighteenth century until its demise in 1967. There are three chapters breaking up the narrative which concentrate on the buildings occupied by the firm. These concern no. 1 Coventry Street, no.12 (later renumbered 13) Swan Street, and finally the historic cellar. The latter is covered separately because it was in fact not under Harveys' premises, but under the neighbouring no.2 Coventry Street. This was leased from 1935 by the wine merchants, who were permitted to break through from their own cellars.

The first chapter includes a brief sketch of the history of the wine trade. The moving of wine up the Severn was well established in medieval times and much of it would have been French wine from Gascony. However, for centuries after the loss of Bordeaux by the English in

1453, the Bristol merchants looked to Spain and Portugal for their wines. After the reduction of tariffs in the early 1860s, French wine was again popular and prominent among the stocks of wine merchants including Harveys. Yet it was to be one sherry in particular which ensured the survival, growth and fame of Harveys. Bristol Cream, believed to have been introduced by 1870, was the forerunner of amorosos, which are rich sweet sherries. It was an immediate success and has continued to be the market leader ever since. Bristol Cream is an example of an early and enduring brand name. It was registered by Harveys as their trademark in 1886.

The business of a wine merchant was undertaken separately in Kidderminster and Bristol for several decades before the Harvey family became involved. The Kidderminster business began c1790 under William Thorn, who came from Bristol. It predated by a few years the Bristol enterprise which was founded in 1796 by William Perry. Later, the key figure was Edward Prichard, who for forty years moved between Bristol and Kidderminster, playing a vital role in introducing the Harvey brothers, John and Charles, to the work which made their name. Although by 1839 the businesses in Kidderminster and Bristol both carried the name of Harvey, they continued to operate entirely separately. This changed in 1912, by which time they had become limited companies. In that year the much bigger Bristol company took over the Kidderminster company bearing Charles Harvey's name.

The last family member to run the Kidderminster company, Lydia Harvey, died in 1950. She probably had a hard time trying to convince Head Office that her branch was worth retaining. Before the Second World War the Board of Directors had already become sceptical about Kidderminster's value to them. From 1955 Harveys started to expand quickly, and this fast growth, with ever greater international exports killed off any chance of the town having a significant role in future plans. Other depots were opened, including one at Rubery near Birmingham. The final straw was the determination of the local council to destroy the premises as part of a major development of the Swan Shopping Centre. Charles Harvey & Co. Ltd. closed in December 1967, and the premises were demolished in 1968.

For the most part, during the centuries covered by this book, wine drinking was a privilege enjoyed by the wealthy classes, and Harveys served the gentry and aristocracy. In his Wealth of Nations published in 1776, the great Adam Smith seemed to regret this elitism, even though he was an advocate of the benefits of free market forces. He commented:

> "... if we consult experience, the cheapness of wine seems to be a cause, not of drunkenness, but of sobriety. The inhabitants of the wine countries are in general the soberest people in Europe; witness the Spaniards, the Italians, and the inhabitants of the southern provinces of France. People are seldom guilty of excess in what is their daily fare... in the countries which, either from excessive heat or cold, produce no grapes, and where wine consequently is dear and a rarity, drunkenness is a common vice, as among the northern nations..."

On the opposite side of the political spectrum, the equally great Karl Marx showed a very active commitment to the benefits of wine consumption. He has left us with the immortal words of advice: "Be careful to trust a person who does not like wine."

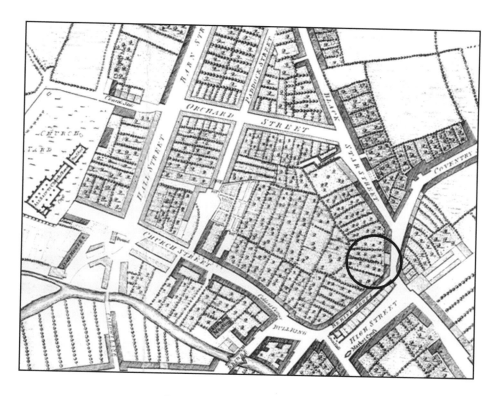

Kidderminster 1753

This extract from Doherty's plan of 1753 must be used with caution. The gardens lying behind the street frontages seem to be extensive, but many of them would have been covered with outbuildings. The angle of the garden boundaries is inaccurate behind the premises which would later be occupied by the wine merchants. The line of these gardens should turn more towards Orchard Street, which itself should be at a line parallel with the top end of Church Street. Nevertheless the plan is useful. The light-shaded rows of buildings in Hall Street, Orchard Street etc, represent Lord Foley's plan for the use of the land which belonged to the manor house he was demolishing. The latter probably stood near the proposed corner of Hall Street and Orchard Street. The plan clearly shows that any "chapel" in the cellars of the wine merchants would have been isolated from the manor house amidst the medieval streets of the town shown by the dark-shaded lines of buildings in the lower right of the picture. Amidst the old town are occasional light-shaded buildings, which probably represent other buildings owned by Lord Foley. These included the Lion Hotel at the top of the High Street on the right of the picture. Just to the left of the hotel can be seen the sharp corner at the top of "Behind Shops" which was to become Harveys premises. Next to it is the light-shaded building which was owned by Lord Foley and later became The Clarence Inn, under which was the legendary chapel-like vault one day to be leased by Harveys.

Chapter One

Early Wine Merchants

In 1964, in his classic History of the Wine Trade in England, André Simon wrote that the origin of the trade was "wrapped in the greatest obscurity". In particular, he doubted there was any proof that the Romans imported wine to Britain during their occupation. More recently, however, historians seem to accept that large jars, amphorae, were used by the Romans for this purpose. In fact, Salway has claimed that Italian wine was coming into this country by this method "in the first half of the first century BC and possibly even earlier".[1] Whatever the truth concerning this early period, it is likely that any organised wine trade ceased for some time after the Romans left Britain. Much later, in the 10th and 11th centuries, it is known that Rouen merchants enjoyed a monopoly of trade in French wines and were seen in London.[2]

The story of Harveys, wine merchants of Bristol and Kidderminster, has its foundation in the wine route from Bristol up the river Severn into Worcestershire. It is not known with any certainty when this began, but the available evidence suggests that it was in the early Middle Ages with the order imposed by various Norman kings after the Conquest of 1066. By the 12th century wine was imported into the port of Bristol in substantial quantities. The Severn was navigable as far as Shrewsbury, and in 1175 a vintner, or wine seller, was recorded in that town. In 1232 Henry III procured wine imported to Bristol for his castles at Worcester, Shrewsbury, Gloucester and Bridgnorth. It is about this time that we have the first known record of the presence of wine in Kidderminster. Henry III stayed many times in Kidderminster between 1228 and 1233. In a talk given in 1935 the local historian A. J. Perrett said that the king "dispatched many letters of state from the town, and after he left he kept up over twenty years of correspondence with regard to the stocking and disposal of the wines he left in the local cellars." Perrett went on to quote a letter of 1233 to the Bailiffs of Worcester. "Contrabreve to cause two tuns of the King's wines at Worcester to be carried to Kidderminster, there to be placed in the cellar of John Biset for the King's use."[3]

The cellar in question was part of the manor house at Kidderminster held for some time by the Biset family, at least until 1280. In his talk, given at a time when Harveys' cellar was exciting great historical interest, Perrett confessed to wondering whether the wine merchants' cellar was the very same Biset cellar. He did rule out the possibility, and so does this book. It is a most unlikely proposition, and there is no evidence at all that Harveys cellar had anything to do with the manor house.

Wine was transported up the Severn by extraordinary wooden sailing vessels called trows, which were designed for commercial river traffic and also sailed from Bristol up the river Wye. It is believed these boats date from the middle ages. They had flat bottoms and masts which were lowered to go under bridges. Their main growth probably took place from the late fifteenth century. By 1756 there were 350 trows trading on the Severn and the Bristol Channel.[4] In favourable conditions trows could sail from the wide estuary near Avonmouth known as King Road up to Gloucester in a day.

There is no doubt that the journeys undertaken by the trows were very hazardous. Navigation was apparently once possible for small boats carrying 40 tons of cargo beyond Shrewsbury to Pool Quay near Welshpool. Even these were 60 feet long. The river is and was very shallow in places, and gangs of men were employed to pull trows upstream to places such as Bewdley. In these upper reaches the passage of the trows was intermittent and relied as much as possible on the high spring tides in a two-week cycle. It is thought that until 1840 the river was tidal as far as Worcester or Upton-upon-Severn. Despite the navigational hazards, by the mid 18th century barges with a capacity of up to 100 tons were plying their trade. From Gloucester the larger ones would operate downstream, while the smaller ones would concentrate on the shallow upstream route. As a class, the trow owners were known for opposing improvements in the river channel. When George III was king, fearful their craft would become obsolete, "they shouted themselves hoarse, and tossed their hats in honour of victory, over the defeat of the first attempts to improve the channel."[5]

Another hazard was the competition between the towns on the Severn, each of which had their own fleet of trows. In 1411 Bewdley men were accused by Gloucester and Bristol traders of not allowing them to pass up river unless they agreed to hire the Bewdley boats. In 1496 the authorities at Worcester were charging tolls on vessels going upriver as well as on goods loaded or unloaded. Three years later, in a dispute with Bewdley, it was decided that no toll should be charged on goods which were simply carried past Worcester. Another complaint of this nature was laid against Worcester in 1563, but after this the city seems to have abandoned its efforts to collect such tolls.

The boats took a range of goods, but mainly cloth and wool, downstream to Bristol. They returned with other goods, including wine, which in 1576, for example, was the principal cargo brought back to Worcester.[6] For much of the Middle Ages the wine would have undoubtedly contained a substantial element of French wine. This trade was facilitated by the fact that the empire of the Norman kings of England contained much of modern France, including the port of Bordeaux from where the Gascony wines were exported. According to Simon, the trade in French and German wines to England was of "greater antiquity" than from the Iberian Peninsular of Spain and Portugal. However, there is no doubt that Peninsular wines were imported to England throughout the Middle Ages. At the end of the hundred years war in 1453, and the loss of Bordeaux by the English, this trade received a lasting boost with regard to Bristol. The established wine route became the Peninsular to Bristol and up the Severn to Worcestershire and beyond. In the early 19th century virtually all the wine imported into Bristol came from Oporto and Cadiz.

Despite the difficulties of navigation, the facility of sending wine so far inland from Bristol via the Severn was of exceptional value to that city. Bristol became, after London, the most important wine market in England. In the 15th century it had become very prosperous. The Peninsular wines coming through the city were often of a sweet variety, but during the 16th century the reputation of the drier sorts became very great. The name sack was used from this time to denote the drier kind, so if we are to be pedantic, Falstaff's appreciation of sack in Shakespeare's Henry IV was a historical error. During the greater part of the 17th century sack was the most popular wine in England. At first the name applied only to the wine produced in the Jerez locality and shipped from Cadiz, but by this time it applied to all wines similar in taste and colour. These included other Spanish and Portugese wines, and even those from the Canaries and Madeira.

In the 17th century, after London, the largest wine-importing ports were Hull, Southampton and Bristol. From Chester wine was sent only as far as Newcastle-under-Lyme. So Bristol continued to be the key port for Kidderminster and the West Midlands. "There was no remote country seat nor inland town where wine could not be easily obtained at a cost only slightly above the London prices."[7] After the Restoration the diary of Samuel Pepys frequently mentioned sack. By the end of the century the name sack was gradually being replaced by the modern sherry, which is derived from Jerez, the most important of the three sherry towns in southern Spain close to Cadiz.[8]

By this time wine was very clearly the drink of the gentry and the aristocracy. The working classes had long since abandoned its use in favour of beer, which was cheaper and readily available with opening up of internal trade due to increasing ease of transportation. Whilst the King, noblemen and others with considerable wealth might have imported their wines directly from abroad or bought it wholesale from English importers, there was considerable retail trade in 17th century taverns, which were used primarily by the middle classes. There was an opportunity for specialist wine merchants, but I have been unable to discover any wine merchants in Kidderminster or Bewdley before 1790. It is likely that Bristol wine merchants had long been arranging direct delivery to wealthy customers in the area, and perhaps to taverns too. We must presume that ordinary wine sellers, or vintners, may have operated in the two towns, but their presence is not conspicuous either. A comprehensive study of Bewdley wills proved locally between 1660 and 1760, for example, revealed only one vintner.[9] It may be that wine was distributed by dealers in general goods who had a suitable cellar for storage.

The wealthier classes tended to have their wills proved in London at the Prerogative Court of Canterbury. Analysis of their occupations suggests that the wine trade expanded sufficiently by the late 18th century for the emergence of many more wine merchants at that time. Prior to 1750 only 36 wine merchants had their wills proved there. These included two at Bristol, but none in the Midlands. However, between 1751 and 1780 there were another 182, including eight at Bristol and one each at Gloucester, Bridgnorth and Shrewsbury. In the following thirty years up to 1810 there was a similar number, 192, which included nine in Bristol, three at Worcester, two at Gloucester and one at Bridgnorth. Clearly there was potential for the introduction of a wine merchant's business to Kidderminster or Bewdley, but no name has emerged before 1790. The Shrewsbury wine merchant, whose probate was in 1764, was Richard Wolley, or Woolley. By what might be taken to have been coincidence, his father Thomas Wolley, also a wine merchant, was the mortgagee in 1729 of the premises at Coventry Street which would later become the base for a wine merchants' business run by William Thorn, the Prichards and then Harveys. The premises and this transaction will be discussed in the next chapter.

William Thorn

William Thorn is the first known Kidderminster wine merchant. The Harveys archives are peppered with references to him as starting the business which became their branch in the town, but nothing seemed to be known about him or his life. Research for this book has revealed much of the man. The business is always stated to have been founded prior to 1790 by him. This date is probably derived from a surviving 1790 Poor Rate List where Thorn appears as an occupier of premises in the locality where Swan Street met Coventry Street.[10]

Almost certainly Thorn came from the Bristol merchant community, and he set up in Kidderminster to take advantage of its distribution potential which had been enhanced by the growth of the canal network in the Midlands and northern England. In Kidderminster the canal had opened in 1771. Born c1758, Thorn married Mary Ann Long in December 1783 in Bristol.[11] It was probably around the time of his wedding when he came to Kidderminster to set up the wine merchant's business. It did not take him long to achieve prominence in the town. From August 1792, when he was elected to the common council, he is regularly mentioned in the minutes of the town council. In October of that year he was among the common councillors who successfully voted for Robert Shirley as High Bailiff. Thorn was chosen for the office of Low Bailiff at the same meeting. In August 1793 he was among those elected unanimously as Aldermen or Capital Burgesses. Considering he was an outsider Thorn's rise had been very swift, and in October 1794 he was elected as High Bailiff, which was then the supreme civic position in the town hierarchy.[12]

For the next seven years Thorn was possibly the most prominent of the citizens of the town. In October 1795 he took the oath to serve as Justice of the Peace, which was customarily taken by the High Bailiff of the preceding year. In October 1797 Thorn was again elected as High Bailiff, and in the following year he again served as Justice. In October 1799 Thorn was a key figure in an extraordinary civic event when Aldermen Colley, Newcomb, Perrin, Lea, Shirley and Cole were all in turn elected as High Bailiff but all refused to serve. The cycle of reluctant bailiffs was broken only by William Thorn again accepting the office. When he finished another year as Justice in the autumn of 1801, Thorn had held office for six of the last seven years.

Thorn seems to have purchased the premises in Coventry Street in June 1803. The conveyance in fact transferred the property to "the use of such persons" as Thorn was to specify "in writing". This unusual wording might indicate that at this time he had lost patience with the civic squabbles of the town and was considering withdrawing from business there. It is possible that he was looking for a younger man to take over the business and that by this date he already had in mind the elder son of a Shrewsbury wine merchant named Prichard. The likelihood is that there was no change until at least 1807. Certainly this process was complete by January 1811, when he was simply described as 'Esquire' in a conveyance whereby he sold the premises to John Ames, Michael Castle and Thomas Castle of Bristol Esquires for £2400.

In the deed of 1811 Thorn was apparently still resident in Kidderminster, but the Coventry Street premises were then occupied by Edward Prichard. In fact, it is likely that by this time

Thorn was living in the parish of Stone just outside Kidderminster. A statement made in 1857 by Josiah Allen, then 64 years old, clearly referred to this period:

> *"I knew and was well acquainted with William Thorn formerly of the parish of Stone in the said County of Worcester Gentleman now deceased and with Mary his first wife whose name at the time of her marriage with the said William Thorn was Mary Long that the said Mary Thorn died about the year one thousand eight hundred and sixteen... and was buried as I have been informed and believe at Bristol."*

Given that Thorn remained an Alderman of Kidderminster until at least 1827, it seems probable that he maintained a residence in the locality. He may also have retained a home in Bristol, and certainly appears to have done so after William Prichard's marriage in 1811, when the business was probably strengthened by his joining his brother Edward. A William Thorn is listed in a Bristol Poll Book for 1812 as a wine merchant living in Montague Parade in the St. James parish. This suggests that he might well have assisted with the supply of wine to the Prichards in Kidderminster. The only known import of wine by Thorn during the period from 1804 onwards is in July 1805 when he took ten pipes of wine from Oporto. So he would have taken most of his wine from other Bristol merchants. Eventually Thorn moved to a neighbouring Bristol street, Kingsdown Parade, where his wife died in December 1815. His links to the Worcestershire town were still strong, because in November 1816 the Bristol newspapers recorded that he was married in Kidderminster to Catharine Spencer of Hurcott Mills.[13] The second marriage to Kate Spencer was confirmed by another part of Allen's statement.

The detail of the remainder of his life is unclear, and there is no further evidence of any involvement in the wine trade. Thorn's continuing career as a Kidderminster Alderman suggests a much reduced link with the town. After 1801 he never again held office, and his name appears only three times from then until 1823 in the minutes of the council meetings. These recorded his attendance to vote in the High Bailiff elections of 1811, 1813 and 1816. In May 1823 Thorn attended as alderman at the election of Lord Ward as Under Steward for the town. He then was present at three successive High Bailiff elections in October 1823, 1824 and 1825. Finally, the 1827 charter granted to the town by George IV included his name among the twelve aldermen.

At some point he and his wife moved close to the centre of Worcester to Pound House in the Tything. It may be that this move to a new permanent home led to his slightly more regular attention to his duties as a Kidderminster alderman. Evidently Thorn had little desire to live in Kidderminster, but a home in Worcester offered his wife the chance to be near her family. There was an age gap of nearly twenty years between them, and he would have expected to die leaving her a widow for many years. The register of deaths shows that Thorn was buried at St Oswalds in Worcester in November 1835. His will referred to their son William, who was still a child, and stated his place of residence to have been Pound House. Thorn Senior's links with Bristol, and indeed the parish of St. James there, are confirmed by his will dated October 1832, proved at London in 1836, in which he described himself as a gentleman of Claines in the County of Worcester.

If later we are to consider that both the Harvey brothers preferred Kidderminster to Bristol, there is no such possibility in Thorn's case. In his will he declared:

> "I desire to be buried at St Oswald's if I die in or near Worcester, if in Bristol at St. James's where I have a brick grave, and if I die at any other place then in the parish where it shall please God to call me. I particularly request I may not be taken to Kidderminster."

Edward and William Prichard

The detail of how the brothers Edward and William Prichard came to take over the Kidderminster business of wine merchants is not known. Both were born in Shrewsbury, in 1783, and 1785 respectively. Their father, also Edward, was a wine merchant of that town, and he died in May 1796 aged 49. It is likely that he was known to William Thorn through their common interest in the transportation of wine up the river Severn. A further connection of the family to the Kidderminster community was provided by the marriage of Edward and William's sister, Emma, to Robert Wylde who by 1805 was the curate at the parish church of St Mary's.[14]

These connections enabled both brothers to marry into a prominent Kidderminster family at a fairly young age. Edward was married in May 1807 in Kidderminster to Nancy Pardoe. In May 1811 William married Rebecca Pardoe, also at Kidderminster. The two women were the daughters of the wealthy carpet manufacturer, Joseph Pardoe, who had died in 1798. He had been tenant of Franche Hall for some years, and his widow, Mary, continued to live there with her daughters until her death in 1803. William and Rebecca never had children. Edward and Nancy were to have at least five children born in Kidderminster by 1814. Only their son, Edward, would outlive their father.

Another connection which facilitated these marriages was probably a close relationship between William Thorn and Joseph Pardoe. When Thorn was first elected to the oligarchy running Kidderminster in 1792, Pardoe was among those voting for him. The latter was by then a very senior figure in Kidderminster affairs, having been elected High Bailiff in 1786 and 1790. The two continued to meet regularly until October 1797, which is the last occasion on which Pardoe is recorded as in attendance. Pardoe had voted for Thorn as High Bailiff in both 1794 and 1797.

Given that William Thorn was a diminishing presence in Kidderminster from 1801 onwards, it is likely that, although they were both young men, the Kidderminster business was gradually relinquished to the Prichard brothers. In the light of their marriages it seems reasonable to suppose that this took place in the period 1807-11. It is likely Edward assisted from 1807, and was probably in occupation at 1 Coventry Street. At the time of his marriage in May 1811, William was living at Welshpool, so it may have been then that he joined Edward in the business. This would have freed Thorn to think about moving back to Bristol. At first the brothers did not spend time in Bristol and would have relied on Thorn or other merchants for their supplies. The importing of commodities into Bristol was undertaken mostly by that city's own merchants. Worcestershire merchants would then obtain their goods from those merchants, but occasionally they would take the responsibility of importing. For example, Samuel Skey & Son imported thirty bags of sumac in July 1791. Skey was a wealthy merchant who in 1787 built the Spring Grove estate, which is now the Bewdley Safari Park. In November 1792 the same company imported two jars of raisins and 198 bags of sumac. In the same month the Worcester wine merchant, Samuel Crane, imported five butts of Spanish wine. From 1814 the Prichards are recorded taking occasional delivery of wine at Bristol. In October of that year William received five pipes of wine from Oporto, but after that until November 1819 there were seven deliveries in Edward's name, four from Cadiz and three from Lisbon. All of these consignments were relatively small, ranging from one pipe or one butt to three pipes. In the 1818 Commercial Directory Edward was recorded as in business at Coventry Street as a wine and spirit merchant. There was a change soon afterwards, with Edward basing himself in Bristol and William remaining in charge at Kidderminster. In 1820 it is William's name which appears in the Lewis Trade Directory at Kidderminster.

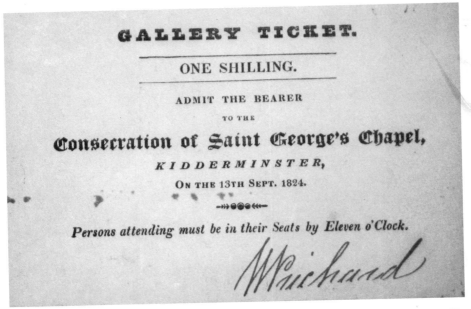

William Prichard's ticket for the opening of St George's chapel in 1824. (BRO)

At this time many businessmen lived on their premises, and it is likely that William did so. Certainly, one of his successors, Charles Harvey, was to do so for nearly fifty years. In those days there was no public bar to disturb the peace of the household in the evenings. Another possibility is that William and his wife lived with his mother. Emma Prichard had followed her three children who had moved to the Kidderminster area. She was a resident of Bewdley in May 1822 when she died aged 73, and was buried in Dowles churchyard just north of the town. It is not known whether she had long resided there.

Meanwhile, the first indication that Edward had started to increase his activity in Bristol was in the 18th January 1819 edition of the Bristol Mercury, which recorded the name "Prichard" by a ship sailing for Rouen in its Ship News. By 1820 he was definitely firmly established there. The Mathews Trade Directory of that year shows him residing in the elegant terrace house at 7 Bellevue in fashionable Clifton, west of the city of Bristol. This was not the mansion of a very rich man, but the home of a merchant on the rise. Also Edward was listed as a wine merchant in the partnership of Castle, Lax and Prichard. This was a continuation of the links between the merchants shown when Thorn sold the Coventry Street premises to three parties including the Castles in 1811. The size of the first consignment of wine imported by the partnership, fifteen pipes from Oporto, showed that Edward Prichard was now operating in a bigger field. However, he remained in this partnership for less than two years. Perhaps he felt their focus was not sufficiently on wine. Between April and September 1820 the company imported two consignments of gin, one of brandy, one of cider, but no more wine.

7 Bellevue, Clifton, is shown in the centre of the picture. This was Edward Prichard's first known home in Bristol.

Urch and Prichard

Perry and Urch was the business which was to give Edward Prichard the opportunity of an enduring partnership. In 1796 William Perry had established himself as a specialist wine merchant in Bristol, and it is this event which gives Harveys their foundation date. In 1806 he went into partnership with Thomas Urch, whose sister Anne had married Thomas Harvey II in 1805. Perry died in February 1820, aged 55, and in due course Edward Prichard became Thomas Urch's new partner, probably in 1821. The first known import by Urch and Prichard was in March 1821, being 20 butts and 2 hogsheads of wine from Cadiz.

In 1822 Thomas Urch's nephew, John Harvey, joined the firm in a junior position. The Harvey family were mariners, not wine merchants. Thomas Harvey I and II, grandfather and father of John respectively, were ship's captains employed by a substantial ship owner and merchant, John Maxse. By the 1820s Thomas II was a man of some substance and was joint owner of two ships, the Bristol and the Feliza. His son by a first marriage, Thomas III, was also a sea captain. Unhappily, the family seafaring tradition was quickly extinguished. Thomas III died unmarried in 1826 at the young age of 39, and in the following year his father died too.[15] The latter's share in his ships was sold by his widow. This left the family's fortunes resting primarily on John.

The company John had joined was facing some difficult commercial decisions. In 1827 a new canal was opened which carried traffic out of the Severn estuary at Sharpness into new docks at Gloucester. This gave merchants the option of importing goods destined for the Midlands directly into Gloucester, instead of down the long Avon gorge right into the centre of Bristol for transhipment onto the Severn trows. These boats occupied the furthest extremity of the Bristol docks, where the river Frome flowed into the floating harbour, requiring a detour from the estuary of six miles in and six miles out. Urch and Prichard must have been tempted to look at a potentially more efficient way of dealing with the wine which they were sending north. Nevertheless, we know they were continuing to use the trows of the Stourport firm, Belsham and Co. for deliveries to the Kidderminster and Bridgnorth area from Bristol after 1827. This company advertised in the Bristol trade directory their trows "by which wines and spirits and other valuable goods are safely conveyed twice a week to and from all places of the North". The business had been a partnership between George Belsham and John Reynolds. Although the latter died in 1811, references to the company often included his name until at least 1827, probably because his wife Elizabeth, who was George Belsham's sister, may have continued to have an interest in the business. An unknown poet, John Tibbitts, has left the following couplet from the year of Reynolds death, which pays a tribute to the honesty of the partners at a time when the pilfering of cargo on the Severn was a common problem:

"While Belsham and his partner Reynolds are
Faithful in freight committed to their care"

Yet it is possible that Urch and Prichard started to import some wine into Gloucester, where the Belsham trows were also operating . In both 1825 and 1826 they imported over 250 butts of wine through Bristol, but the amount seems to have declined substantially in the following years.[16]

Therefore, it was against a background of uncertainty about the future of the port of Bristol that John Harvey worked in his employment for Thomas Urch and Edward Prichard. His move to Kidderminster in 1829 was obviously an important personal opportunity, because he went as a partner and would be able to gain vital experience running the business. It was also important in business terms, because Kidderminster appeared to possess considerable potential as a base for increased wine distribution through the canal network, beyond the usual destinations close to the Severn, deep into the north and east Midlands.

Footnotes

[1]   Salway p457

[2]   A. Simon, The History of the Wine Trade in England (1964). I have used many points from this book. The key references are pp 30, 58, 104, 282 of Vol. 1; pp102, 206 Vol. 2; pp140, 172, 322 Vol. 3

[3]   KS 4.5.1935

[4]   Chris Witts, Tales of the River Severn (1998), p30

[5]   John Randall, The Severn Valley (1862), p246

[6]   Alan D. Dyer, The City of Worcester in the Sixteenth Century (1973), p61

[7]   Simon, op. cit., Vol. 3, p140.

[8]   Julian Jeffs, Sherry (1992), p33

[9]   Bewdley Historical Research Group, Bewdley in its Golden Age (1991), pp202-223.

[10]   KL ref: L362.5094

[11]   The information about Mary Thorn's burial and other biographical information is contained in a declaration made in 1857 by Josiah Allen which is in the possession of the author.

[12]   Two volumes of "Minutes of the Town Council" are held at Kidderminster library for the years 1764-1799 and1799-1828.

[13]   See Felix Farley's Bristol Journal 23.12.1815 and 16.11.1816.

[14]   For this and other information about the Prichards I am grateful to Heather Flack who noted that Robert Wylde first appeared in the marriage register of St Mary's in June 1805 as curate and was still taking weddings at Kidderminster in December 1812.

[15]   Godfrey Harrison, Bristol Cream (1955), pp78-9, 83.

[16]   Bills of Entry held at Bristol Central Library detail the imports. A preliminary study shows for example that in 1827 Urch and Prichard imported only 41 butts of wine, and in 1830 the figure was 72.

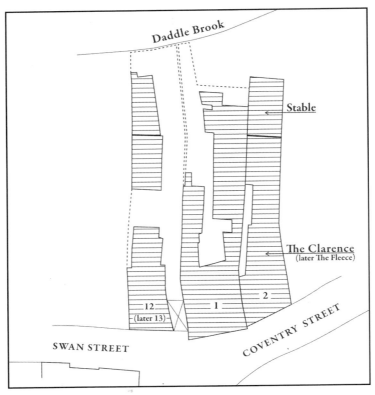

A sketched plan showing the three properties with which this book is concerned. It is based on an approximation of what it looked like in the 1870s when Harveys purchased 12 Swan Street.

A section from the 1885 OS map. Harveys' premises at 1 Coventry Street are clearly marked "P.H.", or public house, even though the ageing Charles Harvey was in residence.

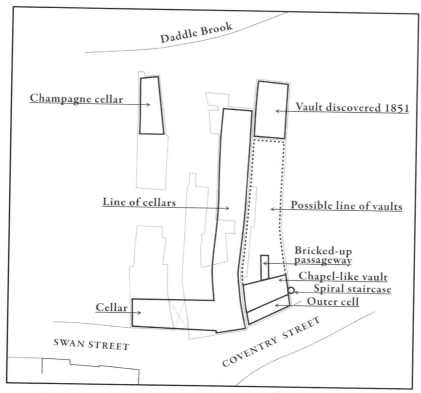

A matching sketch of the cellars lying under the three properties.

Kidderminster Cellars

With the success of its cloth manufacturing, Kidderminster grew strongly in the second half of the 16th century. It is likely that strong cellarage was required for the storing of goods waiting to leave Kidderminster. Goods coming into the town would also have needed secure storage facilities, and these would have included wine. Further study may shed light upon the importance of the town as a trading centre from this time onwards.

We do not know whether the concentration of cellars at 1 and 2 Coventry Street was unusual in Kidderminster. However, Robert Hart has told me that in 1944 he observed a "catacomb of cellars" off the High Street and underneath the indoor market. There may have been a similar network leading down Swan Street from Harveys. This is hinted at by Ian Walker in the notes he made in 1968 before demolition.

One restriction upon the building of cellars was the risk of flooding, which is known to have affected the champagne cellar shown above. Presumably because it was too close to the Daddle Brook.

Chapter Two

1 Coventry Street

This property, where the wine merchant's business was first established, would have been chosen for its cellars. Yet we know little about them. No photograph is known to have survived, nor any detailed record. Instead, the premises are still remembered today in Kidderminster as those which contained the ground floor bar known as "Harveys Vaults". In its last decades, the timber-framed upper floors appeared to mislead Godrey Harrison, who in his book referred to the "Kidderminster building, with its fine old frontage of half-timbered brick".[1] In fact only part of 1 Coventry Street, including certainly the cellars, could have been many centuries old, because there had been at least two rebuilding exercises on the site, and the final frontage of the building was built in the Tudor style in 1901. The cellars did not include the famous chapel-like cellar, which I discuss in later chapters.

The first rebuilding was by Thomas Harris, a chandler. Later deeds, to which I refer below, reveal that his house stood on ground "whereupon four tenements formerly stood". These were pulled down and new buildings erected by Harris. No date is given for this on the surviving deeds. However, when Harveys rebuilt the property in 1901, the modernised premises carried the legend "built in 1699". This fits with what we know of Harris, who would then have been a reasonably young man. His plot was one of the long narrow medieval burgage plots, which had a narrow frontage to Coventry Street. The four tenements must have stood in a line running away from the street. This suggests that the long line of cellars known to have existed at Harveys originally served these tenements. By late 1728, when he made his will, the house was divided into two dwellings, one of which he occupied. After his death a deed of 1729 described the property as having a "large garden walled in with a brick wall, stable, brewhouse, workhouse, backside and appurtenances."

The affairs of the Harris family at this point are a little tangled, not least because there were three generations of chandlers named Thomas Harris. In his will, proved 8th February 1729, the oldest Thomas bequeathed the Coventry Street house to his grandson, Thomas, son of his late son John Harris. However, this was subject to the grandson paying £300 within six months to the middle Thomas Harris, another son of the testator and uncle of the grandson. According to the will this was by way of discharge of a settlement made by the grandfather when he married Alice Baker in 1701. It appears that the old chandler was married three times. The mother of his son Thomas was Ann, and the wife named in his will was called Mary. Given that Thomas the grandson was an adult in 1729 when a deed described him as a chandler, we might suppose that the old chandler married for the first time around 1670. We might reasonably date the chandler's business from that time.

The deeds of 1729 showed how the wishes of the grandfather were given effect by the other two. On the 2nd and 3rd April 1729, still within the six month period set for the grandson to pay, the property was mortgaged to raise £399, with the right of redemption given to Thomas the grandson. Presumably, the money raised was used in part to pay the middle Thomas his £300.

The occupation of a chandler is uncertain. It can be defined narrowly as a maker of candles, or it may be used more flexibly to indicate a dealer in candles and other items such as soap. In fact, it can mean a dealer in a wider range of groceries and provisions. This raises the possibility that wine was among the goods stored by the Harris family in their cellars, particularly as there is no evidence of specialist vintners or wine merchants in Kidderminster at this time. This is suggested by the fact that the mortgagee in 1729 was Thomas Wolley, a wine merchant of Shrewsbury. It may have been that Wolley was known to dealers in Kidderminster, who purchased wine from him which he was transporting up the river Severn through Bewdley.

Because of default in payment, the property became absolutely vested in Wolley. He was dead by 1731 and the property passed to his son Richard Wolley. In 1741 Richard Wolley, wine merchant of Shrewsbury, transferred the mortgage to George Clarke, gentleman of Stourbridge. During this time the Harris family continued to occupy the premises as tenants. One of them was Samuel Harris. Little is known of this Samuel, but he may be the one who was born in 1730, the son of Thomas and Ann. In 1772 a Samuel Harris was among those named as Commissioners to hear cases under an Act passed to ensure the speedy recovery of small debts.[2] It was probably the same Samuel Harris who was High Bailiff of the town in 1776-7. I have been unable to establish when he died, but his death would have provided the opportunity for a new tenant to occupy the premises.

In the Harveys archives it is always stated that the Kidderminster business was established prior to 1790. As stated in the previous chapter, the founder is thought to have been William Thorn, who was in occupation in the poor rate list of that year. Thorn married Mary Long in Bristol in 1783, and it is likely that it was around this time that he moved to Kidderminster after Harris had died. At Coventry Street Thorn was a tenant of the Pratt family. The property had been vested in Henry Pratt of Dunclent in 1769. Henry died c1792, and his brother Thomas Pratt, a gentleman of Stone 'intermeddled' and then died c1794. It was the latter's nephew, James Pratt of Bellington in Chaddesley Corbett, who in 1803 sold the premises to Thorn.

In January 1811 Thorn contracted for the sale of the property to John Ames, Michael Castle and Thomas Castle of Bristol Esquires for £2400. Clearly his contacts with that city remained substantial. At this time Thorn was described as a gentleman of Kidderminster, and in his place Edward Prichard was in occupation of the business premises, which were "formerly made use of as two dwellings". The new purchasers were malt distillers and certifiers, and the purchase money came out of partnership funds. No. 1 Coventry Street in Kidderminster formed part of their business capital and continued to be rented out to the wine merchants. This arrangement continued until 1835 through various changes in the personnel of the partnership. For the purposes of one such change the Kidderminster premises were valued at only £2000.

On 25th March 1835 the Castles finally sold out to William Prichard, late of Kidderminster for £1800. By that time William was described as a gentleman of Cheltenham. The property was then in occupation of Messrs Prichard and Harvey, and in all likelihood John Harvey was living there. In 1841 the will of William bequeathed his dwelling house and premises in Kidderminster to his wife for the rest of her natural life and then to his brother, Edward. Rebecca died in 1848, and so ownership of the premises once again rested with one of the business partners.[3]

Harveys in the late 19th century before rebuilding. We see the sharp corner jutting out into the road where Swan Street met Coventry Street. This was to be removed for road improvement purposes. The picture makes it hard to imagine that the cellars, including those next door to the right at 2 Coventry Street, were once above ground until street levels were raised. It is possible to see through the opening to the yard behind, and it is clear that the land does not drop away. This frontage is likely to be the result of rebuilding in the late 18th century, perhaps after William Thorn took over the premises. (Photo courtesy of Robert Barber)

When Edward Prichard died in 1851, the Coventry Street premises passed to his son Edward, who was a manufacturing chemist in Bristol. By this time Charles Harvey had been living there for over ten years, and he was able to continue there because of an agreement with Prichard that the survivor of them would buy the other share of the business from the deceased's heir. He duly purchased his home in March 1852 from Edward Prichard Jnr. Charles continued to live there until his death in 1889.

The will of Charles Harvey ensured that the premises remained the property of the wine merchants for the foreseeable future. First of all he directed that his sister, Mary Anne, who had lived in Kidderminster with him for nearly fifty years should remain in the property for as long as she desired. She soon moved to live with her relatives at Elderfield, and at the census of 1891 the occupant of 1 Coventry Street was Thomas George, a cellarman aged 32, and his family. He was still there ten years later. Under Charles' will the ownership of the property first passed to his partner James Harvey, and after him to the other partner Frederick Jotham.

The death of James in July 1900 caused a brief obstacle in the Borough Council's plans for the widening of Coventry Street. These had long been on their agenda, and for this purpose the corporation had purchased the neighbouring number 2 Coventry Street in 1884 and numbers 3 to 7 in 1886. In November 1900 an irritated Councillor Bennett proposed the formation of a special committee to negotiate a deal with the Trustees of Harveys' property so that the "so-called improvements may be completed with all convenient speed". However, his colleagues were content to wait. At its meeting on 24th April 1901 the council endorsed an agreement reached with Fred Jotham for setting back his premises. This involved an amended frontage line and compensation of £950 to be paid to Harveys. The rebuilding was carried out later in the year.[4]

No 1 Coventry Street soon after rebuilding in 1901. (BRO)

In 1876 James Harvey had purchased the adjacent property at 13 Swan Street in order to expand the business premises. A boundary wall probably remained for some years between the two properties. The 1885 OS map shows that it was still in place then. In due course, 1 Coventry Street was properly united with the neighbouring premises to create an open yard. The boundary wall may have been removed in the rebuilding of 1 Coventry Street in 1899, as it is not shown on the 1902 OS edition. In 1902 Jotham sold no. 1 Coventry Street to the new company Charles Harvey & Co. Ltd.

The building with its popular bar was closed in December 1967 and demolished in 1968. It is an unfortunate fact that, although we have quite a few photographs of Harveys cellars, none

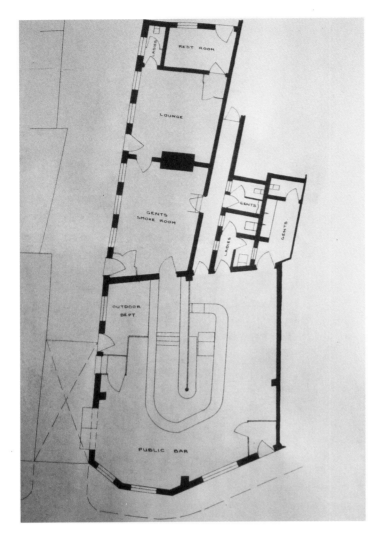

Undated plan of 1 Coventry Street. (Courtesy of John Fudge)

The public bar probably existed throughout the time that Charles and Harriet Harvey, and Mary Anne Harvey, lived there, and perhaps even before. As we shall see in the next chapter, in 1838 the company had a licence for the sale of alcohol to be drunk on the premises. In 1885 the OS map identified the building as a public house.

In its later days the front bar, run by Miss Parkes assisted by Mrs Potter, was immaculate but basic. It was popular with women shoppers, who could enjoy a cup of Horlicks there. Customers could sit on barrels. The rooms to the rear were furnished in more comfortable fashion.

appear to be of those under 1 Coventry Street. These cellars drew the wine merchant, William Thorn, to Kidderminster in the eighteenth century, yet they have been ignored whilst the concentration has been on the supposed "chapel" next door. Their shameful destruction, without any attempt to record them, has robbed us of vital clues to the history of early trade in the town

Footnotes

[1]   Godfrey Harrison, op. cit., p88.

[2]   Rev. John Burton, A History of Kidderminster (1890), p81.

[3]   The apparent decrease in the value of the property between 1811 and 1835 was due to deflation, not to any deterioration.

[4]   The minutes of council meetings are held at Kidderminster Library.

The Severn Trow

The trow is shown here leaving the Bristol docks and turning into the Avon Gorge at the start of its journey to the Midlands. Artistic licence has been used to include the Clifton Suspension Bridge which was opened in 1864. By this time the heyday of the trow was over, and goods would be taken by rail.

Navigation of the Severn was extremely difficult. Occasional underwater rock bars makes the river very shallow in places. Gangs of men, or 'bow hauliers', had to be employed to haul the trows to their destination. This applied particularly between Worcester and Shrewsbury. Even below Worcester and above Upton hauliers were needed if there was no wind. In the 19th century, towards the end of the trow era, the construction of horse towing paths made the hauliers redundant.

Chapter Three

Prichard and Harvey

By June 1829 John Harvey was in Kidderminster. For a short time he was working with both Prichard brothers. However, William withdrew as a partner in October of that year. At 44 years of age he was still young, and his departure may have been due to ill health, as he subsequently lived in two spa towns, Cheltenham and later Bath. This left Edward Prichard and John Harvey trading in Kidderminster as a partnership.

The poor rate list for 1833 names Prichard and Harvey as the occupiers of the Coventry Street premises, which included a "dwelling", so John and his family probably lived over the shop.[1] He behaved as if he believed he would be in Kidderminster for a considerable time, perhaps even permanently. He became a prominent member of the new St George's chapel. In June 1832 £50 was needed to fund an efficient organist and choir. Harvey was among those pledged to fund any shortfall in the monies raised. Like William Thorn before him, he quickly rose to a position of some standing in the town. Although still under thirty years of age, he was chosen to join the self-appointing oligarchy which ran the town, and was to remain an Alderman until January 1836, when he became a member of the new Borough Council as the modest reforms towards greater democracy took effect.

In the centre of this picture is the grave of the three Prichard girls in St Andrews churchyard, Clifton, Bristol. The church was destroyed by bombing in 1940.

Whilst John was getting settled in Kidderminster, it could not be said that his partner Edward Prichard was enjoying a stable personal life in Bristol. He and Nancy lost three of their daughters in a little over five years. Maria died aged fourteen in 1827, followed by Helen aged seventeen in 1831 and Anne aged 22 in 1833. Their surviving daughter, Emma, married in 1829. So Edward and Nancy's move to a much grander tenancy in 1834 had nothing to do with the needs of a growing family. They may have sought to remove themselves from a

Park House, Clifton, in 2010. This is situated on the corner of Richmond Hill and Queens Road. Edward and Nancy Prichard moved here in 1834. They occupied half of this gigantic house

daily reminder of their loss and also to find happiness in accommodation of enhanced status. Their new home, Park House, was still in Clifton, and the poor rate lists valued it at a £33 annual rental as opposed to £20 for their previous home.[2]

Bristol and Kidderminster - Two Companies – Anxiety about Port of Bristol

Although Edward Prichard was a partner in both companies, Urch and Prichard in Bristol and Prichard and Harvey in Kidderminster were clearly separate businesses. However, there was an obvious financial intimacy between the two concerns, because of Prichard's role. The larger Bristol business inevitably treated its Kidderminster counterpart differently from the many other wine merchants it traded with. This is suggested by an entry in a surviving day book covering Urch and Prichard's activity between 1828 and 1833. On 5th October 1829 it was noted that 20 gallons of whisky in a cask and six gallons of brandy in two jars had been forwarded to Prichard and Harvey. The log went on: "Mr Edward Prichard did not mention any price and if we have not charged right the invoice is subject to correction... the brandy is as low in strength as the law allows us to keep it... we have hitherto charged private people 50 shillings a gallon for it, but it is some time since we have sold much of it."[3] Presumably, the Bristol firm did not seek to make much profit, if any, from orders by Kidderminster.

During the years of John Harvey's residence in Kidderminster, the anxiety concerning the future of the great port of Bristol reached fever pitch. In conditions of instability it was by no means certain that Bristol would maintain its importance as a centre for the wine trade. Bristol had been transformed in 1809 by the construction of a new course for the river Avon, which created a large floating harbour not subject to the ebb and flow of the tide. However, the Dock Company which ran the new docks did not invest in the infrastructure for the docks and was widely criticised for imposing charges upon imports well in excess of those set by competitors such as Liverpool. This was not to change until 1848 when the local authority took over.

The disquiet among the Bristol public about the state of their port was expressed in a series of weekly articles by "A Burgess" in the Bristol Mercury from February 1833 to January 1834. These were collected together in one volume in June 1834 and offered to the public at a low price subsidised by "the liberality of some patriotic citizens". The writer felt that the Bristol elite which ran the docks was throwing away the city's advantage for the sake of short-term profit. Concerning Gloucester, he was of the opinion that it could never be a great commercial city despite the improvements. Navigation was dangerous up to Sharpness Point, and ships travelled up the new canal from there at a "funeral pace" to Gloucester, where there was insufficient anchorage. He calculated there was a difference of time in and out of four to five days in Bristol's favour. He went on:

> *"Yet Bristol, with its certain channel, its excellent roads, secure anchorage, broad river, and proximity to the ocean, is absolutely suffering the tortoise to creep by her while she sleeps. By exacting higher rates than the trade will bear, the natural advantages of the port are counterbalanced, and the disadvantages under which the little but growing rival labours, are lost sight of in his superior cheapness."*

The despairing "Burgess" claimed that the typical merchant had "a house at some more favoured port". In his concluding summary, he wrote that Bristol's wine trade was "cut up branch and root". In an extract printed from the Gloucester Journal backing up this assertion, the Bristol Mercury gave figures for the importation of wine from Oporto to four ports in the first three months of 1834. Liverpool took 654 pipes, Gloucester 247½, Hull 176¾, and Bristol only 95¼.[4] All this suggests that Edward Prichard and John Harvey might well have been turning their attention northwards from the ailing port of Bristol.

In fact, whatever truth there was in the claim that merchants were abandoning Bristol, it seems certain that the firms of Urch and Prichard, and therefore Prichard and Harvey, remained committed to their long-established use of the port for their wine imports. First of all, the bills of entry and trade directories for Liverpool show beyond doubt that they had not removed there and were not importing wine through there between 1835 and 1845. Also, a study of the accounts of Urch and Prichard in the 1830s shows that 210 out of 476 identified customers were in south Wales. They had 52 customers in London and 40 in the south west. Of the remainder, 151 were in Gloucestershire and the border counties, whilst 21 were in the Midlands and only one in the north.[5] Clearly, Bristol was the best base for continuing to serve many of these customers. As suggested above, it is possible or even likely that some use of the port of Gloucester was made. Nevertheless, the Severn trows continued to be well advertised in the Bristol trade directory in 1832, and they were undoubtedly still used by Urch and Prichard.[6]

It may be that "Burgess" was exaggerating real problems. Certainly there was no suggestion of terminal decline at the port of Bristol in a jolly letter written in September 1835 to John in Kidderminster by his brother, James, who was evidently working for Urch and Prichard. He wrote: "I have not yet received your order, but perhaps you intend waiting till I set up for myself before you speculate, we have thumping orders from the north so I need not despair of yours yet... there is a great difference between the wine and the timber trades - when wine is imported, only small parcels come and the cargo is divided between many houses." He gave a clear impression of a city which still had many wine merchants. Nothing is known of James' future life, and he was probably the James Harvey who died in Clifton in March 1838.

James' letter also served as a reminder to John of the social attractions of Bristol which he had given up by his move. James told him that the city was "busy and gay at present, there being no lack of amusements, viz. the Fair, Ryan's Circus, Theatre of Arts... the first Necromancer in the World, etc etc. Charles and myself went to the theatre on Friday and saw Romeo and Juliet." He went on to write of their sister Helen. "What do you think of Helen leaving us? She will get bluer than ever being so near our M.P. I hope she will not turn a blue stocking and cut us gemmen out of our philosophical researches." Helen was later to live in Kidderminster, but the exact nature of this move is unclear. The letter is an early example of the conservative views which ran through the Harvey family. There is a hint of fear, albeit masked as a joke about her becoming a blue stocking, that Helen's intelligence might cause some discomfiture for her male relatives. The "blue" theme is also political. James adds some remarks about a visit due from one of England's military heroes. "We expect rather the Duke of Wellington will be here to review the Yeomanry on Durdham Down; I wish you were here to come and help hurrah him. I dare say the Rads will do their best in hissing him, but doubt not the Blues will outdo them."

John Harvey – Tory Councillor

In January 1836 John Harvey was among a large group of Tories who formed the newly elected Kidderminster Borough Council, subject in future to elections by their fellow citizens entitled to vote. Only two of the 18 councillors were Whigs or Liberals. The Tories suffered their first electoral shock in the following November when the Liberals swept the board and ten of them were elected to the council. In the election of November 1837 they were further shocked by the behaviour of the voters, who rejected all six Tory candidates in favour of Liberals. These local Tories evidently belonged to a class of people who believed they enjoyed a right to govern the town. Within days all the remaining Tory councillors, including John Harvey, resigned in disgust. They addressed the burgesses as follows:

"... we had relied for success, on your good sense.... Your conduct however in the hour of trial, has told us that ours was a misplaced reliance; for instead of regarding the just claims of your old and tried friends, you have preferred listening to the calumnies and misrepresentations... circulated... by designing and interested persons.... We cannot but consider the rejection of these highly respectable gentlemen as an affront alike directed against them and ourselves... we have determined to resign from the Council, and have accordingly sent in to the Town Clerk our respective resignations."[7]

Wholesalers and Retailers

The relationship between the Bristol and Kidderminster companies can be further clarified by the account books of Urch and Prichard for the years 1828-40, which reveal that they had over two thousand customers during the period. The rank or occupation of most of them is unknown, but out of 542 who can be classified there were 264 clergymen, 130 servicemen and 32 with titles. Urch and Prichard advertised as wholesalers and there was a minimum quantity they were prepared to sell. For example, concerning spirits, Urch wrote to a lady in Cheltenham that two gallons was the smallest quantity they were permitted to sell. Evidently they had no retail licence.[8] It may be that Urch and Prichard reluctantly stayed outside this type of business because of red tape. On 13th October 1838 The Times reported that a deputation of wine merchants met the Mayor of Bristol who gave this opinion: "That members of the trade who have been allowed the privilege of selling wine and spirits in less quantities than two gallons, are subject to all the regulations of the soldier's billet." The retail trade was covered by a network of wine merchants, about 70 of whom are identified in the accounts as supplied by Urch and Prichard. One of these was Prichard and Harvey in Kidderminster.

Three surviving licences dated 10th October 1838 show the nature of the business of the Kidderminster partnership. They show the small scale of at least part of its activity. The three licences seem to have been renewed annually since at least 1831. One licence permitted Edward Prichard and John Harvey "to exercise or carry on the trade and business of a retailer of spirits, to be drank or consumed in their house or premises (but not to sell spirits to any other retailer of or dealer in spirits)". The cost was £9 9s. It was paid "having obtained and produced a licence for the sail of beer, cider, and perry by retail". No copy of the latter licence has survived.

A second licence permitted them "to exercise or carry on the trade or business of a retailer of foreign wine". The cost was £2 2s. The third licence was a brewer's licence. This permitted them "to exercise or carry on the trade or business of brewers". It was noted no more than 20 barrels of beer were brewed by them in the previous year. The licence cost only 10s.[9]

The handwritten entries in Urch and Prichard's account books are difficult to decipher, but those for sales to Prichard and Harvey in Kidderminster are dominated by port and sherry. All wines have changed their character over time. Port as we know it today developed in the middle of the 18th century as a wine fortified with brandy. The introduction of corked bottles, which were laid on their side and left to allow the wine to mature, helped to make port an extremely popular wine in England by the end of that century, when it was regarded as the national wine. Another wine fortified with brandy, Madeira, also grew in popularity in the 18th century, but suffered a decline in the middle 19th century. Very few transfers of Madeira to Prichard and Harvey are mentioned in the account books. Also listed are some spirits, including mostly brandy itself, but also rum and gin.

The Sherry Era

The numerous sherry deliveries to Kidderminster recorded in the account books confirm that the British sherry trade was enjoying a recovery, encouraged by King George IV. According to Jeffs, the recovery was "rapid, thanks partly to the First Gentleman of Europe, who roundly damned Madeira and swore - by God - he would drink nothing but sherry... Sherry had 'arrived', and soon a decanter was found on every English sideboard."[10] By this time sherry was almost certainly a very different drink to that enjoyed by Falstaff and Pepys. Until the middle 18th century sherry was prepared from wine only two years old. It was sweetened and fortified, but remained thin, feeble, and acid. The production process subsequently changed fundamentally. The modern method involves the extraordinary solera system developed in the middle of the nineteenth century to ensure particular sherries retained a recognisable and consistent character from one year to the next.

A solera is based upon the knowledge that if a small proportion of a cask of superior wine is drawn off and replaced by a slightly younger wine of the same style, the younger wine gradually takes on the quality of the older. A few months later the wine is indistinguishable from what it was before. A solera consists of a series of casks, organised in horizontal rows, whereby the youngest wine in the upper rows is gradually transferred down to intermingle with older wine lower down. The wine to be bottled comes from the casks at the bottom which contain the oldest wine, but not more than one third of the cask is drawn off at any one time. Thus, a continuous supply of the type of wine required for recognised brands such as Harveys Bristol Cream is ensured. It is a wonderful system by which "ghosts of very old wines pass on their genes, as it were, to younger wines."[11]

Even after the wine is drawn off the solera there is more work for the producer in terms of the final blend. Each brand is the result of a particular blend which might involve the introduction of other wines, sweeteners, or the use of brandy to fortify the alcoholic strength. Today's Bristol Cream is a complex blend, which is a trade secret, but is known to contain Jerez's finest wines. These include delicate finos, aged amontillados, and fragrant olorosos, sweetened with wine from the Pedro Ximenez grape.

John Harvey and Edward Prichard exchange places – The Jotham family

The accounts of the Bristol and Kidderminster companies suggest that any recovery in the sherry trade did not happen immediately upon George IV's solemn vow. During the 1830s the profits were at best steady. There is a slight indication that they were actually falling by the end of the decade. This may have been due in part to problems at Jerez which was hit by cholera in 1834. Undoubtedly Edward Prichard and the Harveys would have discussed ways to stimulate the success of their business. In 1839 they reorganised. It may have been coincidence, but for nearly forty years afterwards the profits of the Kidderminster company rose steadily.

The legend, still current at Harveys Kidderminster Office in the 1950s, was that the brothers Charles and John Harvey tossed up for the privilege of taking Kidderminster in the changes which took place around 1840. The story goes that Charles won, and John duly returned to Bristol with his wife and four children. To anyone familiar with both places, this sounds unlikely, and almost certainly there is very little truth in the legend. In the mid-19th century

Kidderminster was not an attractive place. It had suffered the great strike of carpet weavers in 1828, which left the town in a poor state from which it took decades to properly recover. A London reporter wrote in 1849 that 'in all England it would be difficult to find a more thoroughly disagreeable town'.[12] The truth is that Charles probably had personal reasons for being happy to go to Kidderminster. Undoubtedly he would have been visiting Kidderminster from time to time in the late 1830s, both for family and business reasons. He would have met Harriet Jotham, who was later to become his wife.

The Jotham family now begins to play a key role in the story, and was to continue to do so for a further 70 years or more. Alongside John Harvey in the new St George's chapel was a doctor, George William Jotham, who was born in the Wiltshire town of Bradford-on-Avon. The chapel records show that he took expenses in 1834 for a trip to Worcester, and later in the year he was one of four signatories approving the chapel accounts. In May 1838 the Harvey presence in Kidderminster was consolidated by the marriage in Bristol of Jotham to John's sister, Helen Manning Harvey, who may or may not have turned into the fully-fledged blue stocking feared by their brother James in his letter of 1835. They lived at the doctor's premises in Mill Street for many years. They had many children, the first being Helen born in 1839. Their youngest child, Frederick, born in 1853, was later to become a partner in Harveys wine merchant's business in Kidderminster. Harriet Jotham was George's sister. At the 1841 census she too was living in the surgeon's Mill Street household.

This print of an unidentified picture was found amongst the Kidderminster papers at Bristol Record Office. It is believed to be a young Charles Harvey. (BRO)

This second print accompanies the one above. Accordingly it is believed to be of Charles' wife Harriet Harvey (née Jotham) (BRO)

Ultimately, it is certain that the future of the business would not be left to the toss of a coin. Charles Harvey came to Kidderminster, because the needs of the business required a reshuffle whereby John returned to Bristol. The latter's greater experience was going to be needed in Bristol, which was then clearly the more important of the two companies. Thomas Urch was to retire in 1842, and Edward Prichard was approaching 60 years of age. When, in 1839, Urch and Prichard became Urch, Prichard and Harvey, John represented the future of the new partnership for Bristol. Charles did not have the necessary experience of being at the helm. A step up into partnership at Kidderminster was a more comfortable option for him. Indeed, it has been suggested that he had been prepared for the role and John had delegated managing the Kidderminster business to Charles before 1839.[13] The swap between the Harvey brothers was subordinate to a more important swap between John Harvey and Edward Pritchard.

Finally, it is not likely that after ten years as a partner in Kidderminster, John would have allowed a toss of the coin to give his less qualified brother the chance of the far more lucrative partnership in Bristol. Despite the worries over the future of the port, Bristol was obviously a much bigger business than that of Kidderminster. John Harvey would have expected to boost his earnings substantially by the move. The combined earnings of Thomas Urch and Edward Prichard in Bristol during the decade up to 1839 seem to have averaged about £2800 pa. In Kidderminster, John Harvey and Prichard between them averaged about £760 pa only during the same period. These figures represent the incomes of very wealthy men in Bristol and respectable people in Kidderminster. Translated into today's equivalent, Urch and Prichard were enjoying £224,000 p.a. between them, whilst Prichard and Harvey were taking only £61,000.

John had made himself very much part of the Kidderminster community since 1829, and his son Edward was born there in September 1839. Yet these roots were insignificant beside the chance of a return to the native city of both John and his wife with all its social advantages, together with the prospect of considerably increased financial rewards. The move must have been accomplished soon after Edward's birth. By the 1841 census Charles was living at the Coventry Street business premises with his sister, Mary Ann, and a niece, Jane Lowry. Harriet Jotham and Charles were married in 1842.

Everything suggests that at this time Edward Prichard was faltering. If he had still been vigorous and committed to Bristol, then he might well have been able to help either brother establish himself as partner. It is likely that by 1839 Edward's desire to treat Bristol as his home had waned, and it may be that when John Harvey arrived in Bristol it was already known that Edward would return to Kidderminster. His son Edward may already have left Bristol and had certainly done so by 1841. His daughter, Emma, had married William White in 1829. They were his only surviving children. Bereavements must have taken their toll. The death of Nancy, his wife, at the end of March 1840 at their home at Park House, was perhaps the final blow.

Bristol had probably lost its allure for Prichard. It is striking that the notices in the deaths column of the Bristol Mercury persistently referred to him as 'Mr' Prichard. The key to achieving the mysterious standing of 'Esquire' had eluded him. Even his son-in-law, the manufacturer William White, had been given that accolade upon his marriage. The opulence and grandeur of the streets and villas of Clifton may have daily confronted him with some disappointment of his own, as well as constantly reminding him of the hope he once had for his three dead girls. After Nancy's death, he needed companionship, and for a time this may have been satisfied by his sister, Frances, who was shown in the 1841 census at Park House with him. Two servants were the only other members of the household. His Kidderminster connections served him well, and on 23rd August 1842 he was married there for the second time to Mary Reynolds. His new wife, a spinster of Wribbenhall, had been born in 1795. She was the daughter of the late, John Reynolds, merchant and, of course, partner in the business of Belsham & Co., the Severn carriers with whom Edward had long done business.

Edward's family links with the Bristol locality were further diminished when his brother William died in August 1841 at North Parade in Bath. In November of that year, William's widow, Rebecca, made her own will, which displayed a closeness both to Edward and his family and to her relatives in Kidderminster. She had no children, and legacies were left to Emma's son, Arthur White, and to Frances, as well as to her 'dear brother', the carpet manufacturer Thomas Pardoe, and to her sister Elizabeth in Kidderminster. Her plate, linen, china and glass were left to Edward Junior. The residue of her estate was left to Edward, who was made sole executor. Perhaps Rebecca and Edward decided together upon a return to Kidderminster. She was to die in Kidderminster in 1848.[14]

His marriage marked the end for Edward in Bristol. In 1842 he was listed for the last time in a Bristol trade directory, still as a resident of Clifton at Park House, where he had lived since 1834. Thomas Urch retired, and John Harvey duly became senior partner in 1842, when he was joined by another Bristol wine merchant, William White. The company was to trade as Harvey and White until 1871. In that year it was renamed John Harvey & Sons. The role of Edward Prichard in opening the way for John to develop the company whose name would become famous throughout the world had been critical.

John Harvey (1806-1878). He spent a decade in Kidderminster before moving back to his home city of Bristol and giving his name to the business there. (BRO)

The partnership between Edward and Charles in Kidderminster was formalised in 1841, when they agreed to be partners for seven years. They each contributed £2500 capital, just as Edward and John had done previously. They took 5% interest per annum each out of the trading account in respect of this capital contribution. The profits were such that this was never a problem, and indeed it seems clear that their capital was never drawn upon. The premises at Coventry Street were by this time owned by Edward Prichard and appear to have been considered part of the company's assets, contained in the annual accounts under "stock and inventory."

With Edward free to concentrate on the partnership of Prichard and Harvey in Kidderminster, the profits enjoyed by him and Charles Harvey showed a considerable increase on those shared by him and John Harvey. The biggest profit allocated to him and John had been £350 each in 1834. In 1841 Edward and Charles took £450 each. After that the figure only once fell back below that line. In 1846 they took £650. Their success was recognised in a renewal of their partnership in June 1848 for a further seven years. In 1851, the last allocation before Edward's death, they took a huge £900 each. Life for a Kidderminster wine merchant had become quite comfortable. This last figure represents the equivalent of an annual income of approximately £90,000 today.

The grave of Edward Prichard and his mother, Emma, in the abandoned Dowles churchyard near Bewdley. His second wife Mary is also buried here. The river Severn is beyond the field in the background.

The poor rate list for January 1844 shows Edward as tenant of Netherton House in Wribbenhall, where fittingly he could watch the Severn flow by the bottom of his garden. This was a fine property, where he would have lived in some style. It was valued at a substantial annual rental of £46, putting it on a par with some of the detached gentlemen's residences gathered around Kidderminster, but it was not as lavish as some of the bigger manufacturer's estates. In 1844 Netherton House was probably smaller than it was when for sale later, in 1948, as a seven-bedroomed house.[15] Nevertheless, there was considerable wealth in the Prichard family at this time. There appears to have been no pressing financial need for Edward Junior to become involved in the wine trade. He was described as living near Shipston upon Stour in Warwickshire in Rebecca Prichard's will of 1841. In 1847 he set up in partnership with Eden Henry Jones in Bristol as manufacturing chemists. The surviving deeds concerning this enterprise described Edward the younger as "gentleman". The premises at Temple Back were leased from Edward Senior. Jones' father, Eden Thomas Jones, had for some years previously been running a business in the premises, which were known as Jones's chemical works. All the business capital of £2000 belonged to Edward the younger. His new partner clearly had financial difficulties, and ran up debts to the partnership and to Edward the elder. In 1850 the partnership was dissolved, with young Edward paying Jones £1411 for his interest in the good will of the business.[16] It was becoming clear that the Prichards, both father and son, seemed to prefer to commit any capital they possessed away from the wine business.

The 1851 census showed that Edward Prichard, still describing himself as a wine merchant, was continuing to occupy Netherton House. He died in December of that year, aged 68, thus ending the partnership with Charles Harvey. He was buried on 27th December in Dowles churchyard, north of Bewdley, where his mother Emma had been buried in 1822, and where now the gravestones have been overrun by trees and bushes. Thus Edward found his final resting place only a few yards from the great river which had been central to his livelihood.

Footnotes

[1]   WRO ref: BA10470/170.

[2]   BRO film ref: 398/5

[3]   This is on p233. BRO ref: 40913/F/1/1

[4]   The issues of the Bristol Mercury used here are 9.2.1833, 8.6.1833, 4.1.1834 and 7.6.1834.

[5]   Robert Sterling: Harveys of Bristol, wine merchants (1971). This is a university dissertation covering the period 1829-39. BRO ref: 40913/H/1/15.

[6]   The 1832 Mathews Bristol Directory is the first to no longer list the Belsham trows. After George Belsham's death in 1824, the company may have continued for a while in the hands of his wife, Elizabeth Belsham. She died at her house in Stourport in February 1832.

[7]   See Berrows Worcester Journal 7.1.1836 and 9.11.1837.

[8]   Robert Sterling, op. cit.

[9]   Based on 36 gallons a barrel, this works out at a maximum of about 16 pints of beer sold a day. Nothing is known about Harveys beer making activities in Kidderminster.

[10]   Julian Jeffs, op. cit., p61.

[11]   Helen Reid, Lots of Bottle (1996), p97.

[12]   Nigel Gilbert, A History of Kidderminster (2004), p96.

[13]   Bristol Record Office, Catalogue of the Records of Harveys of Bristol(2004), p1.

[14]   It is quite possible that at her death Rebecca was living at Netherton House with Edward and his second wife. Wribbenhall was at that time in Kidderminster.

[15]   For poor rate list see WRO ref: BA10470/201. For sales particulars see WRO ref: BA9526/59.

[16]   BRO ref: 21126/5

Four Old Pubs Of Kidderminster

The Swan Hotel was in its heyday in the middle of the 19th century. It would be very surprising if the wine consumed here had not come from Harveys, whose premises at 12 Swan Street adjoined the hotel's east wall. (KL)

The Black Bull was another substantial pub in Swan Street throughout the 19th century. It stood at 9 Swan Street, only two doors away from the Swan. Whereas its grander neighbour went out of business c1900, the Black Bull survived until the demolition of 1968 removed it and all the surrounding properties.

... Customers of Harveys?

The listed status of the Black Horse Hotel in Mill Street did not save it from closure in 1973 and eventual demolition. As one of Kidderminster's most important coach houses in the 19th century, it would almost certainly have taken wine from Harveys.

The high number of pubs in the town was shown perfectly by Swan Street. The Fox Inn was a few doors west of the Black Bull and stood at 4 Swan Street. Like the Black Horse, it too was a listed building which was nevertheless demolished. Its age, when it was pulled down with Harveys and the rest of Swan Street, was unknown, but it retained a timber-framed structure at the rear.

(The three photos on these pages are all from the Marcus Everall collection held at KL)

Chapter Four

Uncle and Nephew

With no Prichard ready to step into the late Edward's shoes, the story is now properly about the Harvey family. For the next half-century Charles Harvey and his nephew, James, dominate the Kidderminster business, which for the most part operated smoothly without crisis during this period. Like William Thorn and John Harvey before them, both easily found time to be considerable figures in the civic life of the town. They ranked highly among the local Tories. Harveys have a history of allegiance to that party, which continued until the end of the twentieth century. This seems to have been quite natural given their clientele, of which even by 1900 it could still be said that "it consisted mainly of the titled and landed gentry."[1]

After the loss of his partner, Charles Harvey was to run the Kidderminster business on his own for thirteen years or so. The partners had agreed that the survivor of them would pay the executors of the deceased for this share, so in June 1853 the young Edward Prichard duly sold his father's part of the business to Harvey. This doubled Charles' capital in the business to £5000. Interestingly, he paid 10% interest due on his late partner's share for the period since his death. Clearly Edward the elder and Charles had decided that the healthy profits they had enjoyed in the last years of their partnership warranted the doubling of the interest payable to them on their capital. This was nothing to do with inflation, because the four successive years from 1848 until 1851 had been deflationary, and in 1852 there had been zero inflation.

One of the reasons why Charles carried on alone was undoubtedly that the wine trade was passing through a crisis of confidence, and expansion was unlikely. Many considered that the solution to this was an end to the high duties on imported wine imposed by governments for well over a hundred years. In 1852 a campaign was underway for reduction backed by The Times spearheaded by several letters in that newspaper by Thomas George Shaw, a wine merchant and writer on the trade. Shaw observed that since 1707 duties had been "so high as to exclude all but a limited few from its use". He compared the period 1801-10 with the thirty years up to 1852. In the earlier period annual consumption of wine with "half the population and infinitely less wealth" had been greater in quantity. He claimed that since then wine consumption had declined by 46%. Shaw added that the retrograde path being taken by the trade affected quality as well as quantity. He declared:

> "[Wine] has so fallen in character and respectability, that, were it not that there are still in it many honourable gentlemen, one would feel ashamed to be connected with it... there is probably no trade in which there exists such an amount of trickery and deceit... the long habituated taste for falsified and artificially prepared wines.... I have only to refer to the extraordinary picture exhibited in the evidence laid before the committee of what takes place in the docks, and as that is done publicly, what must it not be in many dealers' cellars? This applies both to wine and brandy, and the result is visible in the undrinkable stuff that one usually gets - at enormous charges - in all but first-rate hotels."[2]

Shaw lamented that entry to the trade was difficult for newcomers "in the face of a few capitalists", because of the large amount of capital required. The implication is that men of money, with no commitment to the integrity of wine as a product, were cutting corners. This would have made life difficult for the "honourable gentlemen" already in the trade, to whom Shaw had referred. It is clear that Edward Prichard and the Harveys came into that category. This was a period when they had done well to keep their business ticking over. They had done so, almost certainly, because of their loyalty and commitment to sherry from Jerez, taking their supplies year on year from shipments from Cadiz. Sherry, by contrast with other wines including port, was to maintain its popularity into the 1870s.

Nevertheless, the general malaise in the wine trade did affect Charles Harvey's trade for a while. In May 1851 the trading profit for the previous year had been £1696, but it would not reach that level again until 1861. In 1852 it slipped back to £884. This was also a time when Kidderminster was in the midst of a slump because of the failure of carpet manufacturers to adapt to steam power, the rights to which had been snapped up by their competitors at Halifax. Between 1851 and 1861 the town's population fell by a quarter. The distress primarily affected the working classes, of course, but it might have had some impact on Harvey's middle class clientele. Yet these were hardly straightened times for Harvey, and he continued to pay himself the improved 10% interest on his capital investment in the business.

By 1860 the government was ready to respond to the campaign for the reduction of duties paid on imported wine. Between 1860 and 1862 the cuts made by Gladstone, as Chancellor of the Exchequer, immediately boosted imports, and expansion was to continue into the 1870s. The duties on fortified wines from Portugal and Spain were not reduced so sharply as those on red and white table wines. This may have been due in part to the poor quality of port, according to Shaw writing in 1864. Sherry, on the other hand, continued to be held in high esteem for the time being, and demand surpassed supply.[3]

Up to 1860 annual profits at Kidderminster had only twice exceeded £1500. That was in 1851 and 1858. From 1861 to 1864 Charles Harvey recorded profits of £1728, £1464, £1554 and £1731. Especially in view of the Gladstone reforms, it was clear that the business ought to have a bright future. In 1862 Charles reached his fiftieth birthday, and he had no children of his own. In 1864 his nephew James Harvey (1841-1900) moved to Kidderminster to support him. James was the third son of John Harvey, and had been born in Bristol in 1841 after the family had returned there. He had spent some time in the office of Mr Richardson, an eminent railway engineer of Bristol, before joining with his father in the business of Harvey and White. He was the third member of the Harvey family of Bristol to come to the town, and he was not to be the last. His arrival was just at the right time. Profits soared over £2000 in 1865 and would continue to rise. James was not a partner initially, so the profits were enjoyed at first by Charles alone, and by 1868 he was awarding himself £2000 a year out of them. This level of income is the equivalent of around £180,000 pa today, so Charles was a rich man. Despite their increasing wealth, Charles and Harriet continued to live on the premises at 1 Coventry Street, and they were never to show any inclination to join the middle class exodus to fine villas on the outskirts of town. On the other hand, Charles was soon to show a selfless concern that some of his relatives should be enabled to enjoy this privilege.

Charles Harvey (1812-1889) (BRO)

Charles Harvey, Tory Councillor

By this time Charles had shown himself to be a decent and unassuming man who was committed to Kidderminster's public affairs. He had been elected to the borough council by 1850 as a representative of the north ward. His lengthy service reached its high point in November 1867. He became embroiled in an angry struggle between Tories and Liberals concerning the town's desperate need for a satisfactory drainage system. The Tories were reconciled to the necessary spending. However, there was much opposition because of the cost from the working classes, some of whom were newly enfranchised by the recent Reform Act . The Liberals, including a vociferous George Holloway, were lining up with this opposition. Six out of eighteen councillors were up for re-election. The Liberals ran a slate of anti-drainage candidates who swept the board in the election, although leaving the Tories still in control. The Tory Mayor, Charles Jefferies, was at the centre of the dispute. It was felt by his opponents that he had pressed on with the disastrous drainage scheme of the engineer, Fairbank, with undue haste. A few days after the election on 1st November there was even an attempt on Jefferies' life when a gunpowder device was left on his front door step at Clensmore House.

At the first meeting of the new council the election of the new mayor took place and the intense hostility to Jefferies resurfaced. An embarrassed Charles Harvey was honoured by

42

a Liberal nomination for mayor to replace his Tory colleague. He anticipated this and stood up at the beginning of the business, presumably to make clear he was unavailable. However, Holloway insisted on making his nomination before Harvey could speak. He said:

> *"The gentleman whom I am rising to propose is, I am sure, one who will give the highest satisfaction to the council, and to the borough and burgesses at large, one whose character is unimpeachable, who has passed his life among us, and whose every conduct has met with the approval of his fellow townsmen... I give you the name of Mr Charles Harvey. (Hear, hear and applause.).... I beg to propose as Chief Magistrate for this borough for the coming year, Mr Charles Harvey. (Applause.)"* [4]

At this point Harvey rose to say "there are circumstances of a public and private nature which prevent the possibility of my executing this office". Despite this, another Liberal, John Stooke, insisted on seconding the nomination, and he told the meeting that "if it is the feeling of a considerable number of councillors that he should undertake the office of Mayor, then he ought not to shrink from it."

Harvey then repeated his unwillingness to stand without elaborating on the specific reasons. He added that the drainage issue would require a great deal of attention in the coming year. He therefore nominated Alderman Jefferies for a second term as Mayor. A vote was then taken, but only after some angry exchanges in which Harvey did not involve himself. Harvey won seven votes, all of whom were Liberals, being Holloway and the six recently successful candidates. Jefferies was re-elected with thirteen votes.

Harvey was then appointed Deputy Mayor and also to several committees. He was never to become mayor of the town. Perhaps the episode left a feeling that he had shrunk from seizing his moment. Indeed, it may be that he had already displayed a lack of leadership. In the run up to the election there had been three special meetings where the drainage question had been discussed. At the first he said nothing which indicated a definite view, and he was absent from the later two meetings. After his death it was said of his character by the then Tory Mayor, E. J. Morton that there was a "complete absence of self-assertion or self-aggrandisement." [5] So perhaps deputy mayor was as high as Charles was ever going to rise.

The sorry saga of a town apparently unable and unwilling to provide itself with satisfactory sanitation must be told elsewhere. Suffice it to say that in 1869 a government inspector had to order the council to take action. [6] The ill feeling between the parties on the matter rumbled on for years, and Charles Harvey was one of the early casualties. After the 1867 borough election the Tories still controlled the council, but they had lost the confidence to proceed with the much-needed waterworks and drainage improvements. In their election address for the borough poll of November 1868, Charles Harvey and his five fellow Tory candidates wrote that they had not attempted to implement the scheme "in deference to the expressed wishes of many of the burgesses." They added their belief that the time was "not far distant" when the measure would be demanded. Meanwhile, they unhesitatingly pledged themselves to "the utmost economy. and strictest watchfulness against unnecessary expenditure." This caution worked for four of his colleagues, but Charles failed to be re-elected even though the

Tories did win four of the six seats available. He was not to sit on the council again.

What were the "circumstances" preventing Charles from standing for Mayor? These were a combination of family and business matters. Concerning the latter, his preparation of James for partnership was at a critical stage. Also, it is likely that his wife's brother, George Jotham, may well have been ailing by then. Charles knew he needed time and energy for these tasks, which precluded him from undertaking the demanding role of Mayor. He would have known also that being Mayor would have been very time-consuming. Ultimately, however, even in more favourable circumstances Charles probably did not have enough love of ceremony or status to want the job.

Elderfield in Birmingham Road pictured in 2001

Elderfield and Jotham

In November 1871 Charles purchased Elderfield House with land of over two acres, gardens and 2 cottages for £1700. He did not reside there himself, but purchased it for his relatives, who thus lived in far grander style than himself. Very soon his sister Helen was in residence with her husband George Jotham. On 4th March 1872 Charles wrote to his brother John, who had been a member of St George's church with George Jotham in the 1830s. He told John that things were much the same at Elderfield. Jotham was better than last week. "Does not gain much strength. He goes around the garden with Helen occasionally."

The purchase of Elderfield did not much delay Jotham's death, for he died in May 1872. The newly appointed vicar of St. George's, Rev. F.R. Evans, said of him that he had been "an unfeigning friend, a devoted, earnest and consistent Christian.... He was often found in the byways of the town, striving to influence those who were straying from their saviour."[7] However, the purchase did ensure that a number of female relatives could live with some comfort, despite the loss of the male breadwinner. Helen became head of the household. Two unmarried daughters, Helen and Mary Caroline, still lived with her and were to remain there for many years. They never married. Finally, there was Caroline Jotham, George Jotham's sister, who seems to have come to Kidderminster with her brother and had been living with him there as early as 1841. She too was to remain part of the household for many years and lived to be 95 years old, but her name did not find a place on the Jotham memorial in St George's churchyard. Also benefiting from the provision of such a fine home was Helen's young son, Frederick, who was not yet twenty, but may already have started his four decades of work with Harveys wine merchants.

James steps forward

In 1870 James Harvey took two major steps forward. He married, and became a partner of his uncle, who probably treated him as a son. Uncle and nephew were very different, but there is no record of any discord between them. They probably complemented each other well whilst working together. Charles was solid, cautious and reliable, and did not seek personal recognition of a public kind. By contrast, James seems to have been versatile, ambitious, aware of his own ability and perhaps even a little eccentric.

James married Sarah Goodwin in June 1870. She was the daughter of the miller, Daniel Wagstaff Goodwin, who was a most respected councillor and owned the town mills in Mill Street. They were to have five children, including Charles born 1872, clearly named after James' uncle. The marriage was a good indication of James' individuality and unpredictability, because his father-in-law was a leading member of the Liberal Party in Kidderminster. Although he was never to depart from his family's allegiance to the Tory Party, James never showed any liking for the sometimes hysterical hostility between the two parties which began to abate only at the end of the 1870s.

James was an inventor. He took out a bottle washing patent in 1873, and many years later he was to patent a "pneumatic dusting machine". In the 1879 Littlebury's directory there was a separate entry under James' own name as the "inventor and patentee of the reversing bottle washing machine". The bottle washer was mentioned in March 1984 in a talk to the Kidderminster Historical Society by Joan Harvey, probably the last of the Harveys resident in Kidderminster. She was James' granddaughter. She said that the invention was used extensively in the trade. The machine was turned by hand and involved no soaking or brushing. Scouring was effected by small pebbles in the bottle. She claimed that a workman could clean twenty dozen bottles in one hour. A copy of the patent has survived in the Harveys archive. James described the purpose of his invention as the cleansing of the bottles by the removal of the wine crust and also the scratching of the interior of the bottles so that the crust might adhere more firmly. This was to be achieved by the use of a "proper quantity of spar or other suitable material mixed with water". In recognition of his work he was awarded a certificate of merit at the Yorkshire Exhibition at Leeds in May 1875.

The bottle washer was presumably of great use to the firm of Charles Harvey & Co. The discovery of a surviving bottle with this name on it confirms that some of the wine which arrived in Kidderminster in barrels was bottled for sale, probably to pubs and hotels and other outlets. Many of the bottles were no doubt returned for washing and re-use. Ruby Henderson's mother (Annie Crane) used to recall that when she worked in Harveys bar at the end of the First World War, sherry and port was being bottled by the company for sale to local pubs. This practice never applied to Harveys own branded sherry and port. Bristol Cream, for example, which was soon to be developed by John Harvey & Sons, was always bottled in Bristol.

This wine bottle in the possession of Wayne Bell, shows the name of Charles Harvey & Co. Unidentified liquid remains in it and it is still corked.

With James' entry into partnership the business became known as Charles Harvey & Co. They took profits in the proportion of three to one. So in the year ending 31st May 1871 Charles took £1938 and James took £646. James did not contribute any capital to the partnership. Instead, Charles doubled his own capital to £10,000, which is first shown in the accounts for 1869/70. By this time Charles and Harriet had spent over three decades living at 1 Coventry Street above the business premises. All this time their home had appeared on the accounts as part of the business assets. This practice ceased after 1875/6, partly because fifteen years of growing profits made it no longer necessary to balance the books, but partly no doubt because the purchase of additional premises by James warranted a review of the arrangements.

In December 1876 James purchased the premises next door at Swan Street into which their business would expand. This gave them increased cellarage to store their wine, and they also obtained additional office space on the ground floor. However, until at least 1887 the first and second floors of the new building were let to the solicitors, Thursfields. The new premises were held by James in his own right, and did not form part of the company's business capital.

He let the cellars and the ground floor to the company for a rent which the accounts show to have reached £75 per annum by 1882.

At this time James was clearly ambitious. As well as securing the additional storage facilities for the business, James showed a taste for fine houses at Blakebrook. From his marriage in 1871 he lived as tenant at Hampton House, then number 10 but now number 14. This was next door to his father-in-law, Daniel Goodwin, who occupied the Elms, which was unfortunately demolished after the Second World War. In 1886 James was able to move, again as tenant, to the Grove, which had been occupied for many years by the carpet manufacturer James Humphries. He was to live there for the rest of his life. These were fitting residences for a man aspiring to achieve senior status in Kidderminster civic life.

In 1872 James stood in the borough elections as a Conservative candidate for the South Ward. At this early stage in his political career James was, like his uncle, not disliked by the other side. He was complimented by the Shuttle, which of course supported the Liberals, for a 'sensible' and 'modest' pre-election speech, in which he said that both parties had made mistakes concerning the controversial waterworks scheme. James described the improvements as "absolutely necessary" and it was to the honour of the Conservative Party to have inaugurated them.

The bitterness of the campaign was illustrated by a leaflet issued to the electors attacking the Tory William Crowther, a solicitor, and his family for selling the Mitton sewage farm to the Corporation at a £6000 profit when they were still completing their own purchase of it. The vitriol returned by the Tories forced the Shuttle to denounce them for "dirty, cruel and lying" attempts to blacken the character of George Holloway and for "malignant slanders" against Pemberton Talbot. It was the Tories who were on the run. Amidst the insults, James finished bottom of six candidates in the poll for South Ward poll, well behind the three successful Liberals. The election of 1872 was a watershed in Kidderminster politics. The result was a further swing again towards the Liberals, but this time it was a decisive one. Elections for three of the six aldermen were held every three years, and they were due in 1872. The clear Liberal majority of ordinary councillors, who were elected directly by the public, duly elected three Liberal aldermen to replace Tories. This brought to an end eleven years of Tory Mayors.[8]

In November 1873 James stood again as a candidate in the borough elections, but this time in the North Ward, which was a stronger Tory area in those days than the South Ward. He was unsuccessful once more. This time the election was disfigured by the ludicrous tactic of bogus nominations to confuse the opposition voters. The good name of his uncle was exploited by the Liberals, and James probably suffered because the name of a Charles Harvey appeared on the list of fourteen candidates and collected 90 votes. For their part, the Tories failed to dislodge the Liberal Mayor, William Green, from his seat even though they found three other William Greens to go on a similarly long list of candidates. All this rancour may have deterred the gentlemanly James, and he did not contest the 1874 election. He was finally elected in 1875 when he stood in the South Ward. In this election the Tories won an emphatic victory, taking all six seats, despite the Liberals still trying to make an issue of the cost of the drainage scheme implemented some years ago by the Tories. This converted a substantial Liberal majority into a small majority for their opponents. The Shuttle blamed the working classes for deserting the Liberals and raged against the "ingratitude and fickleness of the mob".

James started his political career quietly, but in the year up to November 1877 he showed an increased inclination to have his voice heard in the council. He attended 16 out of 17 possible council meetings. He showed himself to be financially cautious and conservative in social matters. In February the Volunteer Corps asked if they might use the Corn Exchange for their meetings. James proposed they might have it if they paid for gas, but his colleagues agreed that no charge would be made. In August he resisted the proposal of William Green that a third day should be added when entry to the Turkish Baths was at the cheap rate of one shilling, because they were so crowded on the other two days. James argued that the baths were not paying their way and had been an "enormous expense", and "those who could afford and certainly ought to pay more money, persisted in going to the baths at the reduced prices.... He believed that very few genuine working men ever attended the Turkish baths." Green was ruled out of order, but a month later James backed down, causing some amusement with one councillor expressing regret that William Green was not present to hear the announcement. In March the council was invited to endorse a petition in favour of a bill to legalise marriage between a man and his deceased wife's sister. The Tory mayor, Thomas Tempest-Radford wrongly presumed everybody would be in favour. James thought it was nothing to do with council business. He had only ever heard one argument in favour of the proposed measure "and that was that if a man could marry his deceased wife's sister he could only be troubled with one mother-in-law." Nevertheless the petition was supported by 15 members with 7 against. One of those siding with James was Alderman Goodwin, who evidently was not eager to be troubled by James as his son-in-law twice over.

During this period Charles Harvey, though no longer a town councillor, was still involved in public affairs. In June 1875, probably in recognition of his work with the School Board, he joined the Mayor and three others who accompanied the Town Clerk to Birmingham to present an address to Josiah Mason "elaborately engrossed and illuminated in a handsome bound volume". Mason had recently founded the city's Scientific College, and the address gratefully acknowledged "the very special and favourable regard he has manifested for the interests of his native town in the trust deed".[9] In September 1876 Charles attended a large vestry meeting of St Mary's parish on the cost of the new cemetery. In April 1877 he attended the annual vestry meeting. Earlier in 1877 the annual meeting of the governors of the infirmary reported on a debt of over £321. Ten gentlemen had promised donations, including Charles who gave £25.[10]

Like a firework suddenly bursting into the night sky, James' political career reached a surprising early peak, before fizzling out over the years. In November 1877 he was elected Mayor, as a compromise in the fall-out following another controversial election campaign. The Tories were again dominating local politics, but their victory was somewhat hollow due to the disqualification of all the Liberal candidates in the South Ward on a technicality. Thomas Radford was unable to claim the honour of a third successive term as Mayor, as members of his party uncomfortable with the nature of the victory waved forward the more acceptable candidate. James was nominated by Charles Jefferies, but with no undue enthusiasm. In proposing him Jefferies remarked that "it had long been desired that the uncle of the gentleman he was about to propose should have been elected to the office of chief magistrate. He was sure that Mr J. Harvey was eminently qualified for that office." James was elected without opposition, but evidently he succeeded in part because of the respect felt for Charles.

James Harvey (1841-1900)
For some reason he was sometimes known as "Humpy". (BRO)

James was 36 years old only and had been a councillor for just two years. The Shuttle was sceptical of his early elevation, suggesting that he had some sort of hold on the Tory party. "In yielding to the demands of the Uncle's Nephew to be created Mayor, the Tories seem to have ungratefully passed over the personal merits of Captain Cooke". It commented sarcastically that among the alterations he had in mind was the addition of a "dram and bottle department to his business".[11] It was later said that his year in office "was not characterised by any special features."[12] Certainly, James was not linked with any major political issue. In the campaign for 1876, James had spoken of "the necessity of improved dwellings in the town" and of his desire to put into force the Artisans Dwellings Act.[13] But there is no evidence that he ever contributed significantly to improved housing. We do know that he donated the lime trees planted in Radford Avenue and Comberton Hill in his term of office. Later, he would add trees to the green at Summer Place.[14]

James' term of office ended unceremoniously, made worse by the loss of his council seat as the Liberals benefited from a public reaction to the Tories' ruthless success in disqualifying their candidates in the previous year's election. At the next council meeting William Green moved a vote of thanks to James who, he said, had never indulged in any act of discourtesy. George Holloway objected that the vote was out of order, but after lengthy delay it was seconded. James was going quietly. He commented that he was glad to be "relieved of a good deal of extra work" and that the duties of the Mayor "could scarcely be imagined by those uninitiated".[15] James was soon to be restored to the council, but he would never again be quite to the fore of town politics. In any case, a time was approaching when involvement in local politics was no longer such a priority for the business elite. The introduction of and growth of limited companies was creating more competition, and James knew by the late 1870s that the wine trade was stagnating. The boom was over.

Comberton Hill c1925 showing the lime trees planted by James Harvey. They gave the street an air of urban dignity and prosperity. (KL)

The lime trees at Summer Place near Blakebrook.

These lime trees at Radford Avenue, outside St. George's church, were also planted by James Harvey, as were those above at Summer Place.

Footnotes

1   Godfrey Harrison, op. cit. p120. The connection of the Harvey family with the Conservative party was re-emphasised in 1995 when George McWatters (1922-2007) stood as their parliamentary candidate in the constituency of Bristol South. He was the grandson of Edward Harvey, born in Kidderminster in 1839, and was the chairman of the company from 1956 to 1966.

2   The Times, 28.10.1852.

3   See, for example, Godfrey Harrison, op. cit., p157; and Julian Jeffs, op. cit., p77.

4   Kidderminster Times 30.11.1867.

5   KS 13.4.1889.

6   Nigel Gilbert, op. cit., p112.

7   KS 18.5.1872.

8   For 1872 campaign and election results, see KS 26.10.1872 and 9.11.1872.

9   KS 8.5.1875 and 5.6.1875.

10 KS 3.2.1877.

11 KS 10.11.1877. "Captain" Cooke must have been the Tory councillor Henry Cooke. Ironically, his death was soon to provide James with a further political opportunity – see next chapter.

12 This was in his obituary. See KS 4.8.1900.

13 KS 4.11.1876.

14 See Ken Tomkinson and George Hall, Kidderminster since 1800 (1975), p91, for Radford Avenue trees; KS 5.1.1878 for Comberton Hill; and his obituary KS 4.8.1900 for Summer Place.

15 KS 9.11.1878.

Chapter Five

12 (later 13) Swan Street

Harveys premises in the 1870s were part of a town centre which included many pubs, such as the relatively recent Fleece (formerly the Clarence) next door and the historic Lion Hotel which looked down the High Street only a few yards away. Undoubtedly Harveys supplied many of them with wine and spirits, particularly those establishments serving the wealthier classes. When the company expanded by James Harvey's purchase in 1876 of 12 Swan Street, which adjoined the west side of the wine merchants' original premises, it was buying into a street of great interest including three more pubs, the Fox Inn, the Black Bull and the Swan. It was a travesty when all this was pulled down, along with Harveys, in 1968.

The town centre had grown out of a medieval market square. A row of buildings had developed in the middle forming the High Street on the south side of the square and a street known as Behind the Shops on the north side. The three pubs were all contained in the row which climbed gently to join 1 Coventry Street at the top. In the early 19th century Behind the Shops became Swan Street.

The first known documentation concerning 12 Swan Street is a deed of 6th July 1773. This revealed that in 1766 the property had been mortgaged by a baker from Halesowen, William Goddington, and Sarah his wife for £150 borrowed from Serjeant Hornblower, a Kidderminster mercer. The purchaser in 1773 was a butcher, Joseph Brecknell. He paid £100 to Matthew Thomas, butcher, and the remaining £180 was to be paid to Hornblower, who got his money in October 1774 when the property was finally conveyed to Brecknell.

The property was then described as "all those two messuages standing together in a certain street called Behind Shops having the dwelling house late of Thomas Harris, chandler, on the east side, the dwelling house late of James Goddington called the Swan Inn on the west side, and which said two messuages were in the several tenures of Edward Thomas butcher and John Rogers tayler but now are in the holding of the said Matthew Thomas......And also all those three stables, pigstye and garden to the said messuages belonging and which said stables and buildings are now converted into one stable, a cowhouse, slaughterhouse and a pigstye and are now also in the occupation of the said Matthew Thomas or his undertenants."

It is likely that Brecknell improved the property, converting it into one residence and giving it the frontage which it retained until demolition in 1968. The surgeon, Thomas Bradley, was tenant in 1798 and remained there until his death in 1818. His son, also Thomas, continued the tenancy. He was one of Kidderminster's most prominent citizens, and was High Bailiff three times, in 1831-2, 1834-35 and 1835. He followed his father into the medical profession, and was one of the two surgeons, with Thomas Thursfield, who treated the poor in the original dispensary at St Mary's Street, the costs being met by public subscription. His son, Rev. Edward Bradley, better known as Cuthbert Bede, achieved fame as a novelist with his book, Verdant Green (1854).

This is believed to be the furthest outbuilding behind the Swan Street premises. The loft window at the end would have looked across Daddle Brook to New Meeting chapel.

The wooden truss in the centre of the picture is set in the wall and contains large metal bolts. This suggests goods may once have been hauled into the loft for storage.

We believe a cellar lay underneath this building, so it is a surprise that there was a brick floor. This suggests that there was a change of use in the late 18th century when the surgeon, Thomas Bradley, moved in. The floor may have been strengthened for coaches and horses. (BRO)

During the tenancy by the two Bradleys, ownership of the house passed from Joseph Brecknell through a succession of family members. In 1773 Henry Perrin married Mary Brecknell in Belbroughton. Their son, Samuel Brecknell Perrin inherited the property. He died at the age of 50 in 1828 intestate and unmarried, leaving his three sisters Sarah, Mary and Betridge coheirs. Betridge died in 1847 intestate and Sarah died in 1850. Their relative Lucy Lawrence, born Lucy Perrin in August 1819 and a descendent of the brother of Henry Perrin, obtained the property by conveyance in 1855 from Mary Perrin, who died three years later. Lucy married John Turner Lawrence a joiner of Spring Bank. Their son Samuel was born in June 1852. She died intestate of jaundice in 1870, when she and her husband, then a timber dealer, lived at 64 Park Lane. In September 1875 John Turner Lawrence and Samuel Perrin Lawrence, grocer, sold 12 Swan Street to William Coxon for £1100. By then it was in the occupation of Thomas Lloyd, a grocer who had leased the property since 1856.

On 24th December 1876 James Joseph Harvey purchased 12 Swan Street from Coxon for £1600. The 1879 poor rate list showed that Harveys were in occupation of the ground floor and cellar of 12 Swan Street where they had offices.[1] The solicitor, Alfred Spencer Thursfield, tenanted the upper floors, which Harveys probably never really required throughout their future at the premises. After the death of James Harvey in 1900, the Swan Street property passed to his widow. In June 1902 Sarah Harvey sold the building to the new company, Charles Harvey & Co. Ltd. for £2025. By then its number had changed from 12 to 13 Swan Street, probably because the nearby Swan Inn had been divided into two properties.

The loft space above the outbuilding shown in the picture above. (BRO)

This is the champagne cellar below the outbuildings at the rear of the Swan Street premises. Moët & Chandon was established in 1743 and remains one of the world's largest champagne producers. (BRO)

As time went on 13 Swan Street was properly integrated with 1 Coventry Street with the creation of an open yard so that it was possible to move between the two. The 1885 OS edition, surveyed in 1882, shows a boundary wall still between the two. This was possibly removed as late as 1899 in the rebuilding of 1 Coventry Street. It is not shown on the 1902 OS edition. Some of the outbuildings belonging to the Coventry Street premises may also have been removed during this work. The noisy yard of an expanding business was ultimately not conducive to renting out the upper floors of the Swan Street premises. The solicitors, Thursfield, had moved to 12 Oxford Street by 1896, and it may be that no tenant replaced them. In the end by the late 1950s Mary Lawson recalls that the rooms upstairs were not used for very much, and probably served just to house the office toilets.

The whole of the Swan Street premises, with its cellars, was destroyed with 1 Coventry Street in 1968 to make way for the Swan shopping centre.

Harveys, probably taken in 1957, with 13 Swan Street being the block to the left showing access to the yard at the rear. Some refurbishment had been carried out in that year. (BRO)

Footnote

[1]   WRO ref: BA10470/230b.

Looking into Harveys Yard c1960

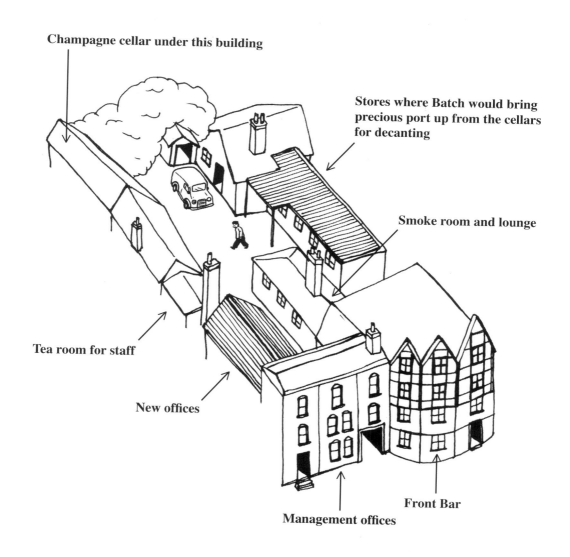

Champagne cellar under this building

Stores where Batch would bring precious port up from the cellars for decanting

Smoke room and lounge

Tea room for staff

New offices

Management offices

Front Bar

Chapter Six

Bristol Cream

The time was coming when the Kidderminster company would be left in the shadow of its Bristol counterpart. The extent of Harveys' business up to c1880 in the historic port has not been properly studied. The Slaters directory for 1880 lists over eighty wine merchants in the city, but many of these would have been small-scale enterprises, which purchased their wine from the importers. It seems reasonable to suppose that as importers Harveys were among the most prominent of Bristol's wine merchants, but not yet outstanding. Soon Harveys was to become an internationally renowned company. In October 1878 John Harvey I died. Having built his career as a wine merchant upon the basis of a decade spent in Kidderminster, it was his work in Bristol which laid the foundations for the future fame of the family name. From 1842 until his death he had been senior partner in the Bristol business, which was at first Harvey and White, then from 1871 John Harvey & Sons.

As for his political career, this had clearly been finished by the 'ingratitude' of the Kidderminster voters in 1837. The Bristol press reported that the late wine merchant "had never taken any active part in political life, but he was greatly respected by a large circle of friends. He leaves behind him a widow and family, two of his sons being Mr Alderman Harvey and Mr E. A. Harvey, municipal representative of St Augustines." This reminds us that a political position was still then an important factor in the status and standing of citizens, even if they had achieved business success. The Alderman was the eldest son, John Harvey II, who was a member of the Conservative party, as was his brother Edward.[1] John II was to become the first chairman after the conversion of the business into a limited company in 1893.

A generation of Harveys was passing. At the time of his brother's death, Charles Harvey was at an age when he might retire. Indeed, it may well be that to all intents and purposes he had handed over daily management of the Kidderminster business to James. A letter has survived dated 19th September 1879 to "My Dear Mrs Harvey" from "your affectionate brother Charles Harvey". In it he referred to 'the dark cloud which overshadowed us all', and it is clearly a letter to his brother's widow. He thanked her for her kind hospitality to him and Harriet during the "many months" they had spent with her at her home at Clifton Park Villa in Bristol. Evidently the business had been left in James' hands while he was away. They had just returned home and he went on to tell Mrs Harvey:

> "Today we have been to St. George's, Elderfield and Bewdley. A fair walk under Spring Grove Wall in going and returning and a pretty walk too but not to be compared with those I so much enjoyed on Clifton and Durdham beautiful downs. Every place however has its own charms and our long residence in this not very aristocratic town has so attached us to it, that many things which to a stranger's eye would be insufferable, to us are comparatively unimportant."

These words display the relatively untroubled character of Charles. He knew that others might think he had given up much by coming to Kidderminster, but he was content.

The blending of Bristol Cream

John Harvey I probably died just before the rise of the brand which one day would lead to the name of Harvey being known across the globe. Legend has it that the name of Bristol Cream was first suggested in 1882. "The name originated when a lady visitor was being shown the cellars by Edward. John, who was there tasting sherries, asked her opinion of two blends. The first was the firm's Bristol Milk, and the second an even finer Oloroso. She was a good enough judge to appreciate quality. "If that is milk," she said, "then this is cream." And Bristol Cream it has been ever since." Yet when they applied to register "Bristol Cream" as a trade mark in 1886, Harveys claimed to have been using the name for about ten years prior to August 1875.[2] It may be that it took time, and many appreciative lady visitors, before Harveys realised the potential of branding the richer sherry called Bristol Cream.

For over two centuries sherry known as Bristol Milk had been available. It was not a brand, and certainly the name belonged to no particular merchant. Anybody could market a sherry with that name. It has been described by Jeffs as "the traditional style of dessert sherry that has been imported for centuries." It was known to be available in Bristol as early as 1643. Fuller's History of the Worthies of England stated: "Some will have it called Milk because... such Wine is the first moisture given Infants in this City." Jeffs, in telling the usual story of Bristol Cream's origins, adds that Harveys "intended to introduce a new dessert sherry blended with an even older oloroso than that in Bristol Milk, but had not decided what to call it." They were pioneering a new category of sweet Amorosos, now usually known as cream sherries. They were based upon high quality solera wines allowed to mature and blended with one of the sweet Jerez wines which used the Pedro Ximenez grape.[3]

The story of the creation of Bristol Cream implies that during the late nineteenth century Harveys used their cellars to experiment with their own blends of sherry. However, once a successful blend was established, it is likely that Harveys immediately arranged for their Spanish suppliers to undertake the work for them according to their specifications. Certainly, this was to be the case for the most part in the twentieth century.

Bristol Cream was to be an extraordinary success for Harveys. It eventually turned them into a household name and was responsible for most of the company's profits. It became the market leader for rich, sweet sherries for many decades into the modern period. It quickly became and remained the choicest of all Harvey's sherries. At a time when the wine trade was stagnating and the sherry boom was over, Harveys at Bristol showed great foresight in registering Bristol Cream as a trade mark in 1886. It was one of the developments which must have convinced Charles Harvey & Co., if they still needed any convincing, that the Kidderminster side of the Harveys business was becoming relatively insignificant.

Charles Harvey ailing – a new partnership

Charles Harvey was ailing for some years before his death. His obituary in 1889 described him as having lived a secluded life owing to the failure of his sight for nine or ten years. By the early 1880s it must have been obvious that James needed help in boosting the business. The decline in the wine trade generally, and in the sherry trade in particular, had their effect in Kidderminster. Profits had reached a peak of £3373 in 1876. In 1881 they had fallen to £2625 and would continue to fall. The main reason for the reduced popularity of sherry was that its quality had been compromised because supply could not satisfy demand. In the 1860s selling sherry was easy and anything labelled 'sherry' could be sold. Some of the wine shipped from Jerez was of poor quality due to the introduction of wines from nearby areas of Malaga and Alicante to cope with demand. Eventually people started to notice, and by the late 1870s merchants realised their customers were giving up sherry because it was not the same drink they had grown used to.[4] In addition there was a sustained attack on sherry for medical reasons beginning in 1873. This was not finally debunked until an article in the Lancet in 1898. Furthermore, the temperance movement gathered steam in the 1880s.

A re-organisation at Kidderminster was formalised by articles of partnership dated 27th February 1882, when Frederick Jotham, Charles' nephew, was admitted to partnership. The document showed that he had been acting as partner since 1st June 1881. Born in 1854, he had probably started working for the company by 1874.[5] It need not be assumed that a career in the wine business was the obvious move for Frederick. However, his older brother, George William Jnr., had already followed their father into the medical profession, and in 1879 was listed as a physician and surgeon at Mill Street. His residence was in George Street at Tolcarn, which he probably built. It is a house of some character and survives today overlooking the lower end of Cherry Orchard. Frederick seems to have trained as an accountant, as he is listed as such in the 1881 census, so he would have been well aware that the company's profits were starting to slide. As with James Harvey, Frederick's entry into partnership coincided with his marriage, which took place in Bristol in September 1881.

The initial agreement was that Charles was to take half the net profits, James took three eighths, leaving Jotham one eighth only. Clearly this did not reflect the work then being undertaken by the partners, but was based in Charles' case on his continuing capital commitment. Frederick brought no capital to the company. In James' case, it was no doubt based simply on a decade already given as a partner. As already noted, the premises occupied by the partnership were not treated as part of its capital, but were rented by them. Charles, as the owner of 1 Coventry Street, was paid £120 per annum in rent. James was paid £70 per annum for such part of no. 12 Swan Street adjoining as was occupied for the business.

Charles was, of course, resident at 1 Coventry Street, and he was described in the document as 'resident partner'. He was to be paid an additional £70 pa for the board and lodging of the servants connected with the business. By this time he was 70 years old, but he gave a commitment that he would "attend regularly at the office and diligently and faithfully employ his whole time and attention in the affairs and concerns of the partnership". Nevertheless comforts appropriate to his advanced age were firmly established. He was to be "entitled to all wines and spirits required for the consumption and use of himself, his household and visitors, and the cost of all coal, gas and candles used in the said residence shall be paid for by the partnership." The partnership agreement was clearly intended to secure his comfort for the rest of his life. Fred Jotham's full reward from the partnership lay in the future.

Charles' generation was gradually passing. His sister and Frederick's mother, Helen Jotham died in 1883. She was followed by Harriet, his wife, who died in May 1884. She was buried at St. George's church in a newly built vault. So for the remaining years of his life Charles' seclusion was complete. By 1888 the original partnership agreement had already been altered, with Charles taking a reduction to three eighths of the profits to allow Frederick an increase up to two eighths. At this time profits stood at only £1818, although for a small company that was still a healthy position. Converted into today's currency it represents a profit of around £178,000, which gave £66,000 each to Charles and James and £44,000 to Jotham. Compared to past glories, this was relatively modest income, although Charles continued to derive huge benefit from his annual 10% received from his capital investment of £10,000.

Charles Harvey died on 5th April 1889 within a few weeks of reaching his 77th birthday. He was buried by the side of his wife in the vault at St. George's. His funeral was attended by three sons of his late brother, John Harvey. A week after his death at a service having special reference to Charles, Rev. F. R. Evans, the Rector of Bedworth and a former vicar of St. George's, preached a sermon concerning his "life and labours". He referred to Charles' long work at the Sunday School. Such was the deep regard for him that a plaque was later erected by his friends in his memory in the north west alcove of the church.[6]

The plaque in St. George's church. (Courtesy of Melvyn Thompson)

Charles had given half a century of his life to Kidderminster. The simplicity of his character had obviously won him widespread affection, extending to his Liberal opponents. The obituary in the Shuttle recorded his support for "every charitable movement or institution in the town". After the failure of his sight his seclusion was such "that the general public hardly knew that he was still among us", but he was still contributing unseen to the life of the town. He had helped Canon Boyle in developing the work of the School Board. He had a "deep human sympathy with his poorer neighbours. He was thoroughly imbued with the old-fashioned idea that the way to show love to the Father we cannot see is to do good to the Brother, whose nakedness and poverty are only too evident."[7]

To the end Charles looked after his unsupported female relatives. His will permitted his sister Mary Anne to occupy the Coventry Street premises for as long as she desired, before they passed to James Harvey and then to Frederick Jotham. The complex will also set up trusts based at least partly upon the property at both Coventry Street and Elderfield, which the trustees were directed could be sold. From the trusts various annuities were to be paid, including £500 per annum to Mary Anne, £100 to his sister-in-law Caroline Jotham and £150 each to his nieces Helen and Mary Caroline Jotham. In fact, the trusts were created based upon Charles' residuary estate of £16,144 and the properties remained unsold, presumably because the beneficiaries preferred to continue living at Elderfield. Mary Anne was able to take her £500, but the fund was insufficient to pay the others their full entitlement. After Mary Anne's death in 1900 there was more than enough money in the fund, and in 1902 arrears were agreed to be paid. Caroline and Mary Caroline died in 1903. This left Helen Jotham at Elderfield, where she had been head of the household at the 1891 and 1901 censuses. The last surviving beneficiaries were Helen and Frederick Charles Jotham, who sold the property to James Trenfield Johnson, a Kidderminster carpet manufacturer, on 15th May 1905. Helen Jotham died in December 1907, aged 68.

Resumption of James' Political Career

James was not long absent from the council. The death of Henry Cooke enabled him to return through a bye election in September 1879. Yet from then on, it seemed that he operated only on the fringe of political power. In a council meeting in December 1881 he was mocked by his fellow Tory, Henry Herring, for not attending committee meetings more regularly. He was never a strong political figure, being associated with no particular policy, and having no obvious liking for attacking the opposition. He was probably more comfortable with his non-political work as a Borough Magistrate, which continued until his death, and as a member of the Board of Guardians, which he carried out until about 1895. In fact, he withdrew as a councillor in 1884 when he did not contest the north ward, and he was not to make a comeback until 1889. This period coincided with Charles' final five years alone at 1 Coventry Street. During this time it is likely that James was solicitous in caring for the man who had given him his career and had shown unfailing generosity to all his relatives.

A few months after Charles' death James, perhaps unwisely, allowed himself a renewed burst of civic zeal. He stood for election in the November 1889 borough election as the Tory candidate in No. 6 Ward, or St John's Ward. His opponent was George Holloway, the veteran

Liberal, who had been a councillor for 36 years. The Tories seemed to rediscover their ability to exploit administrative means to get their candidates elected. In three out of six elections no vote was needed, because the Liberal had to withdraw. James was one of the beneficiaries, and the use of the rules to oust Holloway, or the "old man" as the Shuttle referred to him, was particularly cruel. He was ousted because George Henry Fehrenbach, one of the eight to sign his nomination papers, was listed in the electoral register simply as George Fehrenbach. Clearly James made a judgment that his business was stable and that he had time for council work. He probably felt they could go on for ever serving the clergy and gentry who were their tried and trusted private customers. They did not even advertise in those days. Yet in October 1890 there were several huge front page advertisements in the Shuttle by Anderson & Son of Market Place, Kidderminster, describing themselves as "Wholesale Wine and Spirit Warehouses", who were able to make "special arrangements for supplies to clubs, hotels and innkeepers." This was a side of the wine business which Harveys took on only gradually, and it was not until after the Second World War that they gave priority to supplying wholesalers.

James' motivation to re-enter politics has to be suspect, as it was in the earlier phase of his political career. For him it seems to have been primarily about status. In November 1890 his committee activity on the council was still insignificant.[8] By 1892 he was fifty-one years old and becoming something of an elder statesman in the town. This was recognised in October of that year when he was elected as alderman, a vacancy having arisen due to the resignation of Thomas Tempest-Radford. James was the chosen candidate of the Tory Party who continued to have a majority on the council. James probably then simply enjoyed himself in the role of alderman. There is nothing to suggest he used his position for any significant political purpose. The term of office for an alderman was six years, but James served only three years as he had replaced one who withdrew in mid-term. In November 1895 he retired, with neither he nor his party apparently wishing that he sought a further nomination. His level of involvement in council affairs can be gauged by the figures given of attendance for the year up to November 1894. James had attended 13 out of 19 council meetings, which was rather low, and only 12 out of 47 committee meetings to which he had been summoned.[9]

In his final years one of James' main interests was raising money for St. John's church. In 1895 the Shuttle reported that "the annual social gathering in connection with the St. John's congregation was held in the charming grounds of the Elms and the Grove, kindly placed at the disposal of the committee by Lieut-Col Rowland Goodwin JP and Ald. J. J. Harvey JP." James was the treasurer of the parochial fund. This was the seventh such occasion which had been held, and the average net receipts for the fund from them had been £83.[10]

Also, James was developing a new idea, and in 1893 he patented his pneumatic dusting machine. It was a sort of vacuum cleaner operated by two persons, one of them working the bellows and the other pushing the dust collector from place to place. After his death his invention seemed to have some success. The University of Sydney library used it c1902 for large scale dusting operations. The machine was manufactured until 1927 in Kidderminster.[11]

Concerning business affairs James may well have been coasting. Charles' death was not followed at all by any obvious attempts to develop or change. The premises at Coventry

Street were substantially renovated in 1899, but this was to do with the requirement for street widening rather than expansion or renewal of the business. James was content as long as the business was profitable, and of course, despite the inevitable ups and downs, over the years the business had always been profitable. By the middle 1890s it must have been evident to James that the Kidderminster business was not going to grow very much. The old idea of Kidderminster as an important distribution point was looking outdated. The Bristol company, by contrast, looked to have a healthy future. Certainly by 1895 it had obtained the Royal Warrant, when John Harvey & Sons was listed among the suppliers to Queen Victoria. Its Bristol Cream had been a big success and was to be remarked upon by the Prince of Wales when he cut the first sod of new docks at Avonmouth in 1902. Bristol was turning away from Kidderminster as export markets began to be opened, principally in America. James would have been well aware of the global interests being explored by his brothers. John Harvey II visited America in 1893, when the Bristol enterprise showed its ambition for expansion by becoming a limited company.[12]

Soon James did run out of steam. After his death on 29th July 1900 Sarah, his wife, said that he was in "enfeebled health" from March 1898. She added that he "was able occasionally to go down to business. He did not of late have much to do with the management of the business, but he liked to go down and look through the books." Despite his poor health, he had not been confined to bed until shortly before his death. Sarah had left him in bed late one night, but when she returned she found him on the floor. She assisted him into bed and called Dr. E. H. Addenbrooke. At the inquest the doctor said he had attended Mr Harvey continuously for over two years. "He had been suffering from an affection of the kidneys and other allied ailments. He found him in bed suffering from a fracture of the neck of the right thigh bone.... He went on fairly well for a day or two after the fall, and then congestion of the lungs came on." The conclusion of the inquest was that, although James had been getting weaker in the last few months especially, his death had been caused directly by the accident.[13]

This modest cross marks the grave of James Harvey and Sarah, his wife, in St. John's churchyard, close to the church on its north-west side.

Despite the liking for civic honours shown in his lifetime, his was an unostentatious death. He was buried at the west end of the churchyard of St Johns, where he had been churchwarden there for many years. The newly-built grave was plain with a simple small cross on three square stone slabs. It was the desire of the family that the funeral should be as private as possible, and this wish was respected. It was attended by two of his sisters from Bristol and by his brother, Edward, who had become chairman of The Bristol company following the death of their brother John Harvey II in June. Even his will displayed a desire to dispense with the unnecessary. It was short and to the point, leaving everything to Sarah. There was no detailing at all of his property. He may well have been a disappointed man, having never fully realised his potential as an inventor. As the Shuttle remarked concerning his dusting machine, because of his ill health he "did not derive the full benefit he might have done from the patent". It went on to say that James "was an ardent member of the Conservative Party and of the Church of England, but was not wanting in courtesy and kindness to those who held different convictions. He was an advocate of municipal improvement and for adorning and beautifying public places. The trees on the triangular space at Blakebrook, near St. John's Church, were planted by him and give every promise of keeping his memory green far into the next century."

James' death led to the end of Charles Harvey & Co. as a partnership. For a time there would be nobody named Harvey to run the business, which would continue in another form. Nevertheless, the Harvey family was far from finished in Kidderminster.

Footnotes

[1]   Bristol Mercury 21.10.1878 and 22.10.1878.

[2]   For one version of the story see Godfrey Harrison, op. cit., p106. For trademark see BRO ref: 40913/L/2/2.

[3]   Julian Jeffs, op. cit., pp46 and 248.

[4]   Julian Jeffs, op. cit., pp88-89.

[5]   See obituary of his son Eustace – KS 31.7.1915.

[6]   KS 20.4.1889 and Melvyn Thompson, St. George's: A Waterloo Church (2010), p151.

[7]   KS 6.4.1889.

[8]   KS 15.11.1890.

[9]   KS 20.10.1894 and 9.11.1895.

[10] KS 24.8.1895.

[11] See next chapter for more on the dusting machine. The information about Sydney library is contained in an obscure article dated 1969, found on the internet by googling "Harveys Dusting Machine".

[12] See London Gazette 4.7.1895, The Times 9.5.1911 and Godfrey Harrison, op. cit., p109.

[13] KS 4.8.1900.

Charles Harvey's Box

After Charles died he evidently left this camp box in the Kidderminster office. Later it came into the possession of William Clowes Sadler (1864-1924) who became the office manager. Eventually it passed to his grandson, and then to his widow, Shirley Williams, who has kindly permitted these photos to be taken.

William Cock (1751-1843), who made this writing-desk, was a Bristol manufacturer of some repute. A family record on the internet reveals that Cock sailed to New York to find a supply of mahogany. "Tradition has it that while in New York William made a portable writing desk for George Washington's aide-de-camp General Gage. It had a secret drawer for secret dispatches to England." Charles Harvey's box also has such a "secret" drawer.

Chapter Seven

A Private Company

It would not be true to say that the death of James precipitated a crisis in the running of the business. Frederick Jotham had lost his only partner, but it is likely that during James' illness he had become used to running things by himself anyway. It is probable that he continued to do so for a few years. His responsibilities would have included the detail of daily business. The first known manager would be appointed years later at Jotham's retirement. Meanwhile, it would seem that there were no family members in Kidderminster or Bristol to step into James' shoes. At this time of uncertain leadership Charles Harvey & Co. became a limited company.

At first sight, it is perplexing why Charles Harvey, James' older son, did not step forward. He was 28 years old when his father died and would have been the obvious candidate to join Jotham in managing the business. He was listed in the 1901 census as a wine merchant, and also as an employer, yet there is no other evidence for believing Charles was involved in the business at all. His own daughter, Joan Harvey, did not mention him in a talk she gave in Kidderminster in 1984. His occupation is not mentioned in newspaper reports of his marriage in 1903 or of his mother's death in 1907. No directory lists his occupation, even though he was listed as a resident of Kidderminster until his death in 1957. His marriage was to Margaret Harris, daughter of Herbert Harris, a farmer of Waresley Manor House. The wedding took place at Hartlebury Parish Church, with the Shuttle commenting that Margaret's parents were "well known and deservedly esteemed".[1] Yet it is clear that Charles did not join the farming community. From 1912 until 1928 the Kelly's directory had him living at Haverbrae, Lea Bank Avenue in Kidderminster, but no occupation is recorded. Throughout the 1940s he was living at 47 Coventry Street. These houses, both of which survive, indicate a respectable, but far from lavish lifestyle.

Life as a small town wine merchant obviously held little attraction for Charles. The mystery of how he occupied himself is resolved by the 1911 census. He had acquired his father's patent for the dusting machine and was listed as an employer based at a vacuum cleaner factory. The 1912 Kellys Directory gives the factory address as 11 High Street. The business was known as Harvey Pneumatic Cleaners Co. Ltd. By 1924 the factory was at 91 Coventry Street and business had ceased by 1928, when there was no entry in the trade directory.

Given that Charles was leaving the wine business, there was no reason why a woman should not have joined Frederick Jotham at the helm of his business. It is possible that James' widow did assist. In 1902, in a paper surviving among the company records, it was stated that Frederick Jotham and Sarah Harvey had "for some time past carried on the business of wine and spirit merchants".[2] Yet the lengthy report of James' death and the inquest, where Sarah spoke at length, gave no hint of this. In September 1907 the report of her death in the Shuttle made no reference to her ever being involved in the business. This revealed that she "had been in enfeebled health for some time, and when her two daughters were married earlier in the year she was unable to be present at either ceremony, being confined to her room." The report took care to mention her "kind and benevolent disposition" and remarked that "during the whole of her life she was associated with St John's Church, and contributed generously to all its institutions."[3] Yet it said nothing about her involvement with the firm of Charles Harvey & Co. Her involvement with the business must have been purely in terms of making her capital available. Part of her inheritance from James was, of course, the office at 13 Swan Street. The solution to Sarah's anomalous position had been the creation of a limited company. By this means ownership of the company was separated from its managers. Sarah became an investor. A certificate of incorporation was granted in 1902. The business became Charles Harvey & Co. Ltd.

The Limited Company

There was more to the change than clarifying Sarah's position. The late Victorian period had seen a great growth in registered companies anxious to expand. The Kidderminster business was following that of Bristol in converting to a limited company. John Harvey & Sons Ltd of Bristol had been incorporated in 1893 with capital of £200,000, divided into 1000 ordinary shares and 1000 6% cumulative preference shares, both at £100 each.[4] Clearly, the creation of a limited company in Bristol had been motivated by the reasonable expectation that they could expand. Many of the new limited companies were, however, nothing more than partnerships which had assumed company form in order to acquire the privilege of limited liability. It may be thought this was the case in Kidderminster, where by 1902 the business was very small by comparison with Bristol. Further capital was obtained by the issue of 100 debentures of £100 each, secured by a mortgage on no. 1 Coventry Street and no. 13 Swan Street. The issue was dated June 1902. Holders of the debentures were entitled to 5% interest per annum. The purpose of raising £10,000 capital was probably to clear debts, because there is no evidence of any expansion. Half of the loan would be "satisfied" in December 1917, but the remainder would be outstanding until November 1958.

As part of the transformation the premises could now be owned by the company, which now had legal personality. On 12th June no. 1 Coventry Street, which under the terms of Charles Harvey's will had passed first to his nephew James and then to Jotham, was sold to the company for £5820. On the same day no. 13 Swan Street, purchased by James Harvey and bequeathed by his will to his widow Sarah Burrow Harvey, was sold to the company for £2025.

In addition to the premises, the value of the company included an estimate of £5000 goodwill and £7538 stock in trade. However, there were debts of over £6000. So between them Jotham and Mrs Harvey were due around £14000 for their stakes in the dissolved partnership. They did not take cash. Instead they took shares in the company and became the two directors. The capital was a nominal £15000, divided into 7,500 £1 ordinary shares and 7500 £1 cumulative preference shares. The latter conferred a right of a fixed annual dividend of 7%. Between them the two new directors took all the ordinary shares and 6627 of the preference shares.

The new company did not include new blood at the top, and it seems to have been a one man show under Frederick Jotham. He was 48 years at the time, and the company had a precarious and short-term look about it. Under the Act of 1856 seven or more people were needed to form a company with limited liability. The seven subscribers in this case were all family members, who took one preference share each in that capacity. None of them was going to help Frederick run the company. The seven included Frederick himself and Sarah Harvey. The others were John Noel Harvey of the Grove, clerk, son of Mrs Harvey; Helen Jotham of Elderfield, Frederick's unmarried sister, who was 63 years old by this time; Mary Catherine Anne Jotham, married woman of Linden Avenue, Frederick's wife; Ethel Sarah Harvey of the Grove, daughter of Mrs Harvey; George Frederick Jotham of Linden House, Medical Student and Frederick's son. The company was still a family affair, and it may well be that the future acquisition by the Bristol company was always foreseen as likely.

Frederick Jotham (1853-1931) (BRO)

In 1910 the third John Harvey (known as Russell) became chairman of John Harveys & Sons. New capital was added by the introduction of William Garnett to the board of directors. The Bristol company was ready to expand, and plans were laid for the takeover of the Kidderminster firm of Charles Harvey & Co.[5] The purchase was announced at the Bristol annual general meeting in March 1913. The shareholders were told that the acquisition dated from 29th September 1912 and that the Bristol company was taking profits from that date. At the meeting of March 1914 it was said that three gentlemen had 100 ordinary £1 shares each, qualifying them for directorship of Charles Harvey & Co. Ltd. These included Edward Harvey, who was chairman of the Kidderminster branch, and Captain R. P. Harvey, who had handled the acquisition together. In 1915 it was reported that Mr C. A. L. Harvey now had a substantial interest in the company, and also that he qualified for directorship at Kidderminster. The total investment in Kidderminster by the Bristol Harveys was later stated at the 1920 AGM to have been £15,316. This would appear to have been both shares and debentures, because in future the Bristol company's annual accounts would include profits from Kidderminster consisting of both dividends and interest.[6]

Ad from Shuttle 24.7.1915

The End of the Jothams in Kidderminster

The takeover in 1912 was almost certainly the occasion for the retirement of Frederick Jotham, who according to the Shuttle left "a few years before the outbreak of the war". He was replaced by a full-time manager. This was William Clowes Sadler, born in Kidderminster and educated at New Meeting schools. Sadler was by then in his late forties and had already been worked continuously at Harveys for about three decades. In 1912 Jotham was 58 years old. He had already lost his younger son, George Frederick, who died in 1911 aged only 28. This may have been a factor in encouraging him to retire and leave Kidderminster. Certainly, Frederick was described as "formerly of Linden House, Kidderminster" in the Shuttle report of the second major blow to the family. This was the death of his older son, Captain Eustace Jotham, killed in the First World War on 7th January 1915. Eustace was posthumously awarded the Victoria Cross in July of that year. The citation read:

> *"For most conspicuous bravery on January 7th 1915 at Spira Khaisora (Tochi Valley) during operations against the Khoztaral tribesmen. Capt. Jotham, who was commanding a party of about a dozen of the North Waziristan Militia, was attacked in a nullah and almost surrounded by an overwhelming force of some 1,500 tribesmen. He gave the order to retire and could have himself escaped, but most gallantly sacrificed his own life by attempting to effect the rescue of one of his men who had lost his horse."*[7]

Frederick Jotham received the V.C. on behalf of his son at Buckingham Palace on 29th November 1916, when he was 'honoured', in the words of the Times, to be presented to King George V. Perhaps the honour was the other way round, given that Frederick's son had given his life for his country. Eustace's death has a contemporary resonance as the lives of British soldiers are again being lost in Afghanistan in 2010 for a purpose which is not entirely clear. Ruth Butler and Don Gilbert have already described the courage shown by Eustace at a train accident in 1913.[8] Tragically, his brave life was never again to be put to peaceful use.

After Frederick's acceptance of his son's award, we know little of him until his death in December 1931 at 12 Millington Road, Cambridge. By this time the family were long removed from Kidderminster, and this absence meant the Shuttle failed to give him an obituary. Nevertheless his name was added to the family memorial in St. George's churchyard. Five years later his wife died, and her inscription was to be the last, appended by an unknown hand. After the name Mary Catherine Anne Jotham (1857-1936) are written the words "Far above rubies".[9]

The Jotham grave at St George's church

The War Years

The public bar at Harveys was certainly operating in the later war years, because Ruby Henderson can remember her mother, Annie Crane, talking about working there when she was a very young woman prior to an illness in 1919. She described what sounded like wartime restrictions whereby customers could buy no more than three drinks and only for themselves. Ruby's mother also referred to the practice at the time of receiving sherry and port in barrels, which was then bottled at Kidderminster for supply to local pubs.

For some years head office was delighted with its investment in Kidderminster. In 1915 the documents for the annual report for 1914 contain notes from the chairman's speech which stated that there had been an "extraordinary improvement effected in the profits of Charles Harvey & Co. since we obtained control. For some time we were puzzled by a grave deficiency in the retail department, which was gradually reduced and after April last entirely eliminated; with the result that gross profits have risen 14% since we purchased the concern. I am sorry to say in the presence of so many ladies - it was a case of cherchez les femmes, and we now rely entirely on male assistants." This optimism regarding Kidderminster was still evident in March 1919, when in his annual report the chairman went so far as to say that the Kidderminster subsidiary had proved "a veritable gold mine". The balance sheets showed the steadily increasing profits. In 1918 the Bristol accounts included income of £3,803 dividends and interest from its Midlands subsidiary. This increased sharply to £6,745 in 1919. The post-war slump eventually took hold, and the figure went down to £4,033 in 1920. This was nevertheless a good return on the Bristol company's investment in Kidderminster of just over £15,000.

Ad from Shuttle 31.3.1917

Captain Charles Harvey

The annual report of 1919 also revealed that Kidderminster was now being visited every week by Captain Charles A. L. Harvey, who had already made several valuable friends. Charles was the grandson of John Harvey I, and his father was John's fourth son Charles Octavius. From his Bristol base Captain Harvey presided over renewed investment in the Kidderminster premises. At the Bristol AGM in March 1921 it was reported that Kidderminster's turnover in 1920 had been successful and that its "new premises are completed and are to be opened on Thursday". The work involved is not recorded. The most likely possibility is that there was no longer any one living on the premises at 1 Coventry Street and that an opportunity had been taken to refurbish the building, including the bar. It is possible that the upper rooms were removed at this time, replaced by a flat roof behind the retained gables, which is the structure shown in photographs from the 1950s and 1960s.

The front bar at Harveys Wine Vaults photographed by Workman in 1967. (BRO)

As with James Harvey and Frederick Jotham, the prospect of advancement in business for Charles went hand in hand with marriage. In December 1921 he married Lydia Fletcher in Bristol. He was 37 years of age, two years older than his wife. She was the widow of a barrister, who had died in 1916. She was also a Roman Catholic who had been educated at a Taunton convent. Her family lived at Westbury-on-Trym on the north side of Bristol. Her father, Thomas Lindrea, was a leather merchant who died in 1910. Charles and Lydia left Bristol to run the Kidderminster branch in June 1922. They were able to live in fine style, purchasing the late 18th century mansion, Ismere House, at a Birmingham auction in May 1922 for £3750. This stands on the north side of the road from Kidderminster to

Stourbridge near Churchill. Charles had raised £7000 by way of mortgage on the property by May 1923.[10] He and Lydia were to run the business until her death in 1950. They had no children, and it may well be that from the outset Lydia played a leading role. Unfortunately for them, by the time they arrived at their new home there were already signs that Bristol's optimism concerning Kidderminster was becoming tempered.

These two pictures were probably taken during or just after the sale of Ismere House by Lydia Harvey in 1939. The house is shown above. The photograph of the car has "Mrs Harvey" written on the back. (Courtesy of Sarah Houle)

The parent company's sales, which had fallen at the start of the war, had recovered well by 1918, during which net sales were just under £100,000, an increase of over 40% on 1913. The slump came, but in 1922 turnover was over £122,000 with gross profits of £36,000. The chairman, Eddie Harvey, in his annual report given in March 1923, made clear that times were hard. He warned that "the expenses are too heavy and must be reduced." Concerning their subsidiary he went on to say "Kidderminster is doing well and with Mr and Mrs Charles in residence I expect a great increase in business, though at the moment things are quiet there." There seemed to be just a hint of a threat in those words.

The enthusiasm of head office concerning Kidderminster started to abate. Under pressure, the directors adopted a "drastic" policy of reducing stocks to the lowest possible level. This enabled the parent company to show an increased profit in 1923 on a reduced turnover of £111,000. Kidderminster's turnover, despite the new arrival of Mr and Mrs Harvey, was down by over £3000. Furthermore, the income for the parent company from Charles Harvey & Co. was only £1,006. In 1924 the figure went up slightly to £1,169, but it was no longer a substantial part of the Bristol company's overall profit. The annual report given at the AGM in April 1927 showed the first real dissatisfaction with the comment that "disappointing" results from Kidderminster and Portsmouth had prevented record profits. For the year ending 28th February 1927 John Harvey & Sons Ltd had shown a gross profit of over £40,000, of which Kidderminster had contributed a mere £809.

Ad from Shuttle 11.7.1931. This looks like a good bargain during the Great Depression. At today's prices 20/- would be about £51.

Times were changing. Harveys was being forced to gradually modify some of its practices. They could no longer rest on their laurels delivering bulk supplies of wine to established private customers. Increased ease of travel for the middle classes, who dined at restaurants more often and wanted to be able to purchase a bottle or two of wine when they wanted, compelled the company to consider supplying wine to caterers and wholesalers if they were to be certain of maintaining a good position in an expanding market.[11] Yet it was a gradual process, and we shall see that several decades later there was still an emphasis by the company on dealing directly with their private customers as against working through wholesalers. The strong relationship of the Kidderminster branch with long-standing private customers undoubtedly ensured its survival for the time being, but it is likely that Charles and Lydia Harvey came under pressure from Bristol to increase profits.

In addition to worrying about the profits, Charles and Lydia had to deal with the sudden death in April 1924 of the branch manager William Clowes Sadler at the age of 59. His funeral was attended by the Bristol chairman, Edward Harvey, and by Fred Jotham, returning to his native town. Sadler, the loyal servant of the company, was eventually replaced by another man who was to give similar service. Edwin, or "Dick", Warder began to work for Harveys at Kidderminster soon after the first world war as a travelling salesman. He became manager of the branch in the late 1920s. His son, Trevor, who was born in 1923, can remember a boyhood impression based upon conversations between his parents that Charles Harvey did not get on well with his Bristol counterparts. This indicates that he was under strain because of the constant demand from Bristol for greater profits for its shareholders. The reality of this pressure was later revealed in a letter of 1943 which stated that "for years Mr Eddie has advocated disposing of the business, that is to say long before Mr Charles's death".[12] It is likely that Charles' work in Kidderminster during the years of Edward Harvey's chairmanship, from 1919 onwards, must have been marred by argument regarding the viability of the Kidderminster subsidiary.

Outer cell taken by Brooks c1935, shows the ramp through the opening which Harveys made to their premises next door. (BRO)

Cellarage Expansion

Charles obviously managed to hold his own in battles with head office, and on 6th March 1935 Charles Harvey & Co. Ltd. expanded its capacity by taking a lease of the cellar under the neighbouring premises at 2 Coventry Street. The term was for 21 years. The property was described as 'all that cellar or underground room situate and being beneath a messuage shop and premises known as number two Coventry Street... now void together with the right of the tenants to make an underground entrance or way from their adjoining premises into the premises hereby demised but expressly excepting from this demise all other means of access'. Charles immediately showed an awareness of the historical intrigue and the legends concerning this cellar. In August of the same year he invited the Kidderminster Field Club to visit the cellar, and this occasion is covered thoroughly in the next chapter.

Members of the Harveys family and the Board of the Bristol Company in 1937. The occasion was the celebration of fifty years in the firm of Eddy Harvey shown here in his straw hat, which he always wore for work. The man in the light suit at the back is believed to be Captain Charles Harvey of Kidderminster. (BRO)

Charles Alfred Leech Harvey died suddenly in October 1938. He had been at his office, apparently in good health, on the Monday evening, but died in his sleep the following morning. He was only 54.[13] Lydia did not remain long on her own at Ismere House after her bereavement. In April 1939 she sold the house to Mr R. C. Watts for £3500. At the time of this sale the estate contained 32 acres of land. The sale did not make Lydia a wealthy woman. She retained only £250 of the purchase money, and the remainder was paid to the mortgagees. For a time Lydia then lived at Elmhurst in Blakedown

As far as Bristol head office was concerned, it is likely that after the death of Charles the Kidderminster branch was not treated with any serious attention. He was replaced as director by Bertie George Thomas Wright of Bristol, joining Jack Harvey and Phillip Evers-Swindell of Bristol. So for a time the business was, in theory, run entirely from Bristol. Eventually, on 23rd May 1940, Lydia was made a director, and this seems to have been a temporary measure.

Clearly, she had a difficult task. During the years of the war, trade was badly affected. In addition the nature of the wine trade had drifted away from private customers buying in large quantities. This trend had gathered pace from 1918 onwards. Harveys were forced to adjust to selling to wholesalers and caterers, who supplied the growing numbers of customers who purchased small quantities of wine intermittently. This implied a new network of distributors. Harveys travellers were covering the country from end to end. Increasingly Kidderminster's relevance as a key distribution centre was in question.

Footnotes

1   KS 12.9.1903.
2   This is among the records obtained from Company House by the author.
3   KS 21.9.1907.
4   The Times 3.10.1960.
5   Godfrey Harrison, op. cit., p126.
6   For the minutes of a series of AGMs see BRO ref: 40913/S/1/1 and 40913/S/1/2. Captain R.P. Harvey was killed in action in May 1915.
7   For Eustace's death see KS 16.1.1915. For Jotham's departure see KS 19.4.1924. For citation see KS 31.7.1915.
8   Ruth Butler and Don Gilbert, For Valour: Kidderminster's Four V.C.s (2000), p11.
9   These words are taken from the Book of Proverbs 31.10: "A capable, intelligent and virtuous woman, who is he who can find her? She is far more precious than jewels and her value is far above rubies or pearls."
10   I am grateful to Sarah Houle, the current owner, for access to her Ismere House papers.
11   Godfrey Harrison, op. cit., p136.
12   This letter is discussed at greater length in the final chapter.
13   KS 29.10.1938.

View from Church Street c1700

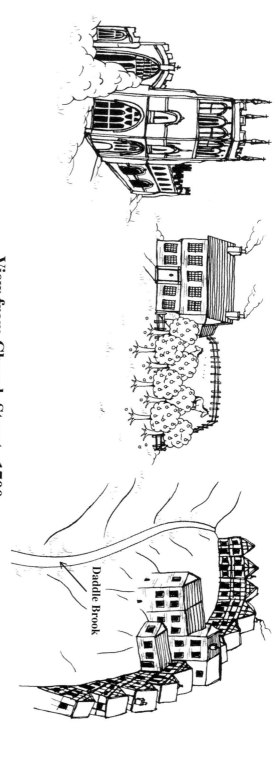

This is an imaginative drawing, as we cannot know exactly what the town looked like in those days. The picture is designed to show key features relevant to this book. In 1700 virtually all the town houses would still have been timber-framed. We have not attempted to show any oubuildings except those behind nos. 1 and 2 Coventry Street. A hint of brickwork is given to no. 2 because we know that the vault underneath was built with bricks.

The short drop of the land down to the Daddle Brook allows us to suggest little basement windows in the last building behind no. 2. This is to show that windows in the vaults were compatible with them being built predominantly underground.

The drawing shows the obvious difficulty of building a "secret" passage from Harveys' vaults to the church. It would have been very long, and any engineer would have had to face the obstacles of the Daddle Brook and the steep bank on top of which the orchard grew.

We have shown the brick-built manor house facing west, but we know little about it and it may well have faced south. The drawing suggests also the unlikelihood of any Lord or Lady of the Manor choosing to build a chapel across the brook amidst the town houses.

79

Chapter Eight

The Vault

The legendary vault amidst Harvey's cellars has excited recorded historical speculation for over 150 years, continuing to do so even after its destruction. Often regarded as a chapel, attempts have been made to link it with various great houses, a Saxon monastery and possible Catholic persecution. The complex of cellars has often been said to extend far and wide, and perhaps incorporating a secret passage northwards to St Mary's church or even south-west to Caldwall tower.

There has long been a belief in Kidderminster that Harveys' vaulted cellar had been a chapel of some antiquity. However, when Victoria Bryant, one of Worcestershire's archaeologists, showed pictures to Professor John Blair, an expert in ecclesiastical architecture, he was "virtually certain that it is domestic, and the undercroft of a late medieval merchant-status house".[1] Having spoken with two of Victoria's colleagues and studied what has been written about the cellar during the last 150 years, I must conclude that it was a merchant's cellar, although the date remains problematic. Nevertheless it remains true that such a cellar, many centuries old, was of great historical significance for a town which was to achieve international fame because of its trade and industry.

The cellar, which was to be later associated with Harveys, had already excited interest for many years before a newspaper report of 1851, and it continued to do so until its gratuitous destruction for the development of the Swan Centre in early 1968. There is a locked door leading underneath the modern complex. When I started the research for this book, I was able to explore this area with Nick Hughes, the chairman of the Civic Society. The rising ground eventually met a concrete barrier, and we were unable to reach the location of the old cellar, which is approximately under the south west corner of Boots. I continued to harbour hopes that the vault had simply been filled in, and one day it might be revealed by archaeological excavation. These hopes were partially dashed when I read an unpublished article by Ian Walker, who had been able to do some brief work in the short period between closure and demolition. It contained the following sentence: "Sadly, our investigation ended when the top half of the vault was pushed over by a bulldozer and the site levelled off for the Swan Centre to be built."[2]

The contempt for the town's history shown by the 1960s council was inexcusable when they had the example of their late nineteenth century predecessors, who took care to preserve the cellar in a redevelopment of that time. Their destructive act has left us to analyse written records and photographic evidence. Although it has been suggested that the cellar was late medieval or Tudor, the best opinion now is that it was late 16th or early 17th century in its origins. There is nothing to support the idea that it was part of the cellars in which Henry II left his wine in the 13th century, or that it was linked to a possible Saxon monastery. We should also discount the legend of a secret passage to Caldwall Hall. There is no evidence for it, and it would have been a considerable engineering feat to take such a passage under the Stour. Similarly there is no evidence for a passage or even a simple network of cellars extending across to St Mary's Church. This too would have posed severe technical difficulties in terms of getting under and waterproofing against the Daddle Brook, which flowed across Blackwell Street immediately behind Harveys and adjoining properties before crossing Church Street. The natural line of any such passage under the brook would have then brought it deep within the sharply rising hillside now held back by a ten-foot wall behind New Meeting, which rises further to Orchard Street. It is difficult to imagine medieval engineers taking on this task. The hill could only have been avoided by sharp turns left and right which would have taken the passage under New Meeting chapel built in 1782. However, there are no known cellars there, apart from a small one underneath the chancel extension, completed in 1879.

Despite the rejection of such legends, we are left to contemplate that until recently there existed a network of cellars which, had they survived, would have given us substantial evidence concerning the growth of Kidderminster into an important industrial town. The surviving documentary material certainly points to a line of vaults extending behind this vault at no. 2 Coventry Street for at least fifty yards or so towards New Meeting chapel. This was matched by another parallel line of cellars underneath the original Harveys premises at no. 1 Coventry Street. Their destruction was unforgivable.

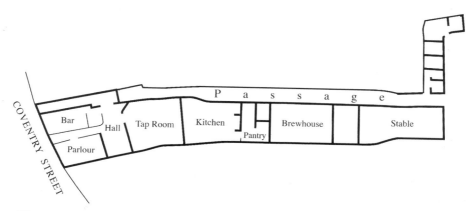

Plan of the Clarence 1871. (From deed held by Wyre Forest District Council)

The Clarence Inn of 1851

As stated in the introduction, the celebrated and much-photographed vault did not lie under Harveys premises at all. Instead, it lay underneath the neighbouring property, no. 2 Coventry Street, which in the nineteenth century was a pub called the Clarence and later the Fleece. It was not occupied by Harveys until 1935. The earliest documented sale was in 1805, when Lord Foley sold it to Mary Broad and Catherine Broad for £635. It was described as "all that messuage dwelling house malthouse yard garden and premises" which for some time had been in the occupation of Samuel Lea. Lea is listed in 1798 poor rates, but not in 1790, when it was the name of James Cole which was next to that of the wine merchant, William Thorn. In 1869, when a nephew of the two women, Charles Broad Ball, sold the property for £600, the stables mentioned immediately below were described as "formerly a malthouse".[3]

The earliest clear written reference to the cellars is a newspaper article of 1851. The Worcestershire Chronicle reported:

> *"The cellars of the Clarence Inn, near Swan Street, in this town, are arched and orna-mented in the ecclesiastical style, and it is the popular opinion that there is a vaulted passage underground leading to the old church. From the character of the windows and mullions it would appear, however, to have been part of a small chapel, and that the street had been raised, and the modern building erected over it. On Monday, while some repairs were being done to the flooring of the stable, it gave way, disclosing a crypt beneath, with a depth of at least two feet of decayed animal matter and human bones. The vault is about eight feet high, allowing for the depth of the deposit, and faces the back of Swan Street. There is every probability that it is only one of a series of vaults reaching from the house in the direction of the New Meeting. The nature of the ground would lead to the supposition that the road in front of the Clarence Inn has been raised several feet, and that if excavations were made some very interest-ing relics of ancient Kidderminster would be brought to light. In the meantime, many hundreds of persons have been to examine this ancient charnel-house."*[4]

Clearly, by 1851 the cellars of the Clarence were already well known and the belief that they constituted a chapel had taken root, even though the writer betrayed a hint of scepticism by referring to their "ecclesiastical style". It is interesting that the plural is used, implying that more than one vault already existed, and these are distinguished from the new discovery. Therefore, this was a previously unknown vault, located under a stable building behind the pub. A plan of the Clarence in 1871 shows the stable to have been the last building in a long line stretching back from the main building fronting the street. The chapel-like vault was close to Coventry Street, as we shall see later. It is reasonable to suppose that there was a line of vaults extending between it and the new vault. Writing in 1905, Ebenezer Guest recalled the accidental discovery. He said that William Fawkner was undertaking some work on his premises at number 2 Coventry Street when he noticed that when his horses pawed the floor in the stables "at the back of his house it sounded hollow and took up the floor and found spacious room underneath, dry and convenient five or six feet below the causeway."[5] This piece by Guest is useful because he wrote about both the cellars at number 2 and those under Harveys at number 1. Commenting on the latter, he said that they extended right back under Harveys property to reach the Unitarian chapel. This, of course, was New Meeting, and it may have been the considerable length of these cellars which gave rise to the legend about an underground passage to the church. If we are right about a line of vaults extending back from the supposed chapel under the Clarence, then Guest's article makes clear that there was a parallel line of cellars very close to them underneath Harveys original premises at no. 1 Coventry Street.

A running issue relating to the vaults is whether they were originally cellars at all. This is raised clearly in 1851 by the reference in the newspaper article to the street having been raised "several feet". Furthermore, in his recollections of the discovery of the vault below the stable Guest wrote that "there was a good sized stone shafted window from which the ancient dwellers must have looked down upon the traffic of their day."

Further Interest in 1850s: George Roberts and Benjamin Gibbons

Interest in the vaults continued during the 1850s. There are three relevant entries for 1856 contained in the diary of the multi-talented George Edward Roberts (1831-65). Born in Kidderminster, Roberts was a draper, natural historian and geologist. He was a Fellow of the Geological Society and moved to London in 1860. On 20th September 1856 he was introduced to Mr Theodore Galton of Hadzor who was preparing material for a paper to be presented "in our Antiquities of next Thursday". Roberts went with him to Fawkner's Crypt. On 25th September, the day of the presentation, he wrote that further research on the crypt was advised. On 11th November Mr J. Severn Walker called on Roberts, who took him to the see the crypt. They agreed an opinion as to date, being late Norman (Transition) circa 1170. They also noted the "ambry" (a recess in a church wall in which sacred vessels are kept, usually near an altar) under the two-light window in the "first" vault. Most subsequent opinion is for a later date, and also there is here the tendency, which others were to follow, to interpret features as ecclesiastical with no supporting evidence. But this latter entry is important because it clearly implies that there was more than one vault.[6]

In 1859 Rev Benjamin Gibbons, then the curate at St George's chapel and later the Vicar of Stourport, wrote of the vault in his Notes and Suggestions for a History of Kidderminster, continuing the assumption that it was a chapel and also suggesting an early date. He described it as "a little relic of ecclesiastical architecture, apparently much - very much older than any portion of our present House of Prayer." His description indicated that he had entered from the possible line of further vaults stretching away on the north-west side of the chapel-like vault. Gibbons wrote:

"You enter by a semi-circular arch, which might from its shape be either Norman or Saxon, into a small apartment with a vaulted roof; on the left side is a small doorway, now bricked up, leading into a passage which has not been lately explored. A semi-circular-headed window opposite to you, now filled up with mullions of the style of the 15th century dividing it into two lights, shows an inner cell into which you may enter by another half-circular arched doorway. This is divided by a wall obliquely pierced by a hagioscope or opening in the wall through which, before the blessed Reformation of religion in this country, persons used to behold the elevation of the host at a neighbouring alter."

Gibbons' description is problematic. There is some ambiguity as to what exactly is divided by the wall, and it is not possible to recognise what he was referring to. Subsequent opinion, starting with Rev. Dr. McCave, preferred a later date for the vault's origin.

Rev James McCave's Articles 1876

In 1876 Rev McCave, the priest at the Roman Catholic church in Coventry Street, offered the first substantial analysis, which is recorded in two articles from a defunct Kidderminster newspaper, The Sun. He visited the vault in the company of one of Kidderminster's outstanding architects, J. T. Meredith, who produced a report with a sketched plan, which McCave quoted from and was to be "laid before the reader in its proper place" McCave was critical of Gibbons and wrote:

"The building is neither Saxon nor Norman, nor so old as the present House of Prayer. The brickwork, the moulded bricks, and the use of the segmental arch over the credence, prove the relic to belong to the first portion of the sixteenth century: the passage is scarcely a passage, but a winding staircase, which conducts to the room overhead."

Picture by Muriel Robinson 1968 - shows a row of arches on left through one of which Gibbons presumably entered. The numerous openings fit in with McCave's reference to "two or three passages". They also raise the possibility of a passage running "alongside the cellars" noted by an observer in 1967 before demolition. (See below.) (KL)

However, McCave continued the assumption that the building was a chapel. His description is quite precise:

"That interesting relic, as was remarked, belongs to the earlier portion of the sixteenth century, and besides the chapel-compartment, which is seventeen feet in length, by fourteen feet in breadth, there is a small outer cell, adjoining the public street, of the dimensions ten feet by ten feet. A number of steps from Coventry Street led down to that cell on the right; and whilst one of the walls of the cell was pierced obliquely, to admit air and a little light, in the wall separating the cell from the chapel was constructed a neat Gothic window, with mullions of the 16th century architecture. As usual the site of the altar pointed towards the east; a little piscina, and a Gothic credence were introduced in order that Mass might occasionally be offered there,

and finally a spiral staircase, from the room overhead, enabled the priest to descend to the chapel without interfering with the cell."

The complete confidence that the architectural detail fits that of a chapel may be explained by the natural bias of priests. McCave unconvincingly suggested that this structure constituted a prison cell with adjoining "gaol-chapel". He noted "the remains of two or three passages, conducting to the chapel", and he speculated that there had been other cells and that the Town Hall might then have stood in Coventry Street.

The south wall of the supposed "chapel" contained features which some observers interpreted as evidence of a religious sanctuary. These openings lead through into the outer cell into which McCave descended from the street in 1876. This photograph is by Brooks c1935, and by then access from the street had been permanently closed as a result of street improvements carried out by 1901. (BRO)

Taken together, the comments of Roberts, Gibbons and McCave convey the impression that there was no doubt that the main vault was a chapel. Both Gibbons and McCave refer to an altar, although they give no evidence of remains confirming its existence. Roberts interpreted an opening in the wall as an ambry for sacred vessels, but it might just have been an opening in the wall. McCave identifies both a piscina and a credence without clearly stating where they were or offering a description showing why he identified them as such. A piscina is a stone basin with a drainage channel for carrying away water used in rinsing the vessels employed at Mass and washing the hands of the priest. A credence is a table or a shelf on the south side of the sanctuary of a church, near the altar, where the sacred elements were placed before the Oblation. Many years later Mr Hodgkins would make the same observations. Yet they were both vague in their descriptions, and Hodgkins may just have been following McCave. It may be that McCave was inclined to interpret the small recess in the south facing wall, which Roberts claimed was an ambry, as a credence. There is much speculation here, and it may be that we must seriously consider the possibility that the vaults were not part of a chapel or other ecclesiastical building at all.

Nevertheless, McCave's contribution is particularly important. He helps us to get our bearings. As well as giving us the dimensions of two compartments, he made clear that the when we look at the photographs of the wall containing the mullioned window with the arched doorway to its right, we are looking southwards towards the Coventry Street frontage. Beyond it was a smaller room into which, and this was one of the most important of McCave's observations, access could be had by steps directly from Coventry Street.

McCave also gave what he presents as a quote from Meredith's report. No copy of the report has been discovered so this is all we have of the observations of a respected architect:

> "... it does not date further back than the earlier part of the 16th century.... It is built entirely of brick partly moulded, with moulds of that date.... The use also of the segmental arch over credence, and the four centre arch to roof, and almost an elliptical arch over the small window would incline him to place it later still, but for the bit of good hollowed work on the brick jambs."[7]

Redevelopment whilst saving the cellars 1901

A long period followed until 1935 without any obvious sustained interest in the vault. In fact, it seems to have been somewhat forgotten. This would have been partly because rebuilding had removed the steps giving access from the street. The Clarence Inn had been renamed the Fleece in 1872, before being acquired by the Corporation in 1884. Two years later nos. 3-7 Coventry Street were acquired also by the council for the purposes of street improvement. This certainly included widening the street and may have included raising its level. The proposed changes had to wait many years. Harveys held on to their property at 1 Coventry Street which extended out by a few feet from the adjoining 12 Swan Street. Eventually they carried out their own improvements to fit in with the council's scheme. Their new premises were suitably in line and carried the legend 'built 1699, rebuilt 1901'. By early 1902 a new row of buildings, numbered 2-6 Coventry Street, had been erected next to Harveys by the contractor, William Woodward Stevenson.

It is significant that the historic vault was left intact even though 3-7 Coventry Street was sold to the developer on condition that "he will forthwith take down all buildings whatsoever erected upon the land". The Fleece was treated differently. The developer was obliged to take down only "those buildings as now stand between the present street frontage and the new building line".[8] This meant that the main chapel-like vault and anything behind survived. All that was removed was the front part of the "outer cell" described by McCave. Evidently the town council of 1901 had a greater commitment to their heritage than their successors of the 1960s. The front walls below street level were to be left as retaining walls and the council covenanted that "it will fill in the space between the retaining walls and the front walls of the new buildings and will widen the existing roadway and pave the pathway within six months". Thus, the street access to the vaults was removed.

This photograph was taken by Fortens in 1957. It is the view from the outer cell described by Rev McCave looking through into the proposed "chapel". (BRO)

Harveys' Lease 1935: New Interest from A. J. Perrett and E. C. Hodgkins

On 6th March 1935 Charles Harvey & Co. Ltd. took on a lease of the cellar under the neighbouring premises at 2 Coventry Street. The term was for 21 years. The lessor was Ernest Paul Ernest Esq. of 163 Bristol Road, Birmingham. The property was described as 'all that cellar or underground room situate and being beneath a messuage shop and premises known as number two Coventry Street... now void together with the right of the tenants to make an underground entrance or way from their adjoining premises into the premises hereby demised but expressly excepting from this demise all other means of access'. Provision was made for the new tenant to block up the existing entrance with a brick wall at their own expense. At the termination of the lease the tenant was to remove any such brick wall and restore the cellar to its former state.

The lease by Harveys led to immediate new interest in the cellars. A. J. Perrett, gave a talk in 1935 where he confessed to wondering if Harvey's were in fact occupying John Biset's cellars, where wine was stored for the use of King Henry III in 1233. The same thought occurred to E. C. Hodgkins in August of that year, when he led members of the Kidderminster Field Club in a visit to the vaults at the invitation of Charles Harvey.[9] Hodgkins said that "possibly in those cellars were stored the wines for the King's use when visiting Kidderminster hundreds of years ago." Yet there is no evidence to support this idea, and neither Perrett nor Hodgkins seriously developed it. The manor house stood close to St Mary's church on the high ground on the other side of Daddle Brook from Coventry Street. The historian, Nash, in 1782 wrote that it had been a "handsome brick house near Kidderminster church (which was very lately pulled down)".[10] His admiration suggests that he had seen it himself. A building called the "Old Hall", marked on the Broadfield map of the town in 1859, is believed to have survived the demolition. It stood behind the houses on the north side of Hall Street on the corner of St Mary's Street, and it was the subject of a proposed deed of gift by its owner John Watson in 1881. However, according to Ebenezer Guest in 1905, Watson had pulled it down because the council had irritated him by asking him to undertake repairs. Apparently, the building had "a large showy sun-dial with gilded letters". Guest recalled that McCave had told him that it was the kitchen of the great hall. In 1890 Burton, who thought that it was likely that the manor house stretched along the north side of Hall Street, wrote: "Sir Edward Blount resided at the Hall close to the churchyard - the last remnants of which have recently been pulled down. When the Savings Bank in Hall Street was built, the workmen found extensive vaults or crypts of solid masonry below, but all was covered up again without investigating." Perrett preferred to think that the manor house occupied the nearby top of Arch Hill. Either way it is not credible to suggest that the Coventry Street vault was once part of the manor house cellars.[11]

The report of the visit led by Hodgkins in the Shuttle referred to the 'subterranean chapel recently discovered in the midst of Messrs Harveys' wine cellars', indicating that the vault had been forgotten for a time. Hodgkins described the place they were standing in as a "chapel or crypt" which had been a "puzzle to antiquarians". His eagerness to embrace the chapel theory, despite lacking evidence of any substance, was the equal of any of the previous observers. Furthermore, with a similarly inadequate foundation, he appeared prepared to accept the theory that the "chapel" was once above ground.

Hodgkins suggested: "It seems reasonable to suppose that, as the street leading to the town bridge was four or five feet below the level of the present street, a fact disclosed by excavation, and helped by the presence of the low lying part of Messrs. Hepworths, the printers, and by the excavations for the rebuilding of Messrs. Boots' shop, the chapel we are now looking at was once above the street level, and was a properly built edifice, not meant for a vault. It is ecclesiastical in character with mullioned window, a majesty, or saints' niche, a picina or credence table. Thus looking to the altar in the east, we have in the south-east an aperture or squint through which worshippers in the sub-chapel in the south could view the high altar through which worshippers could pass from one part to the other."

Not for the first or last time the old vault had provoked a very shaky analysis from an observing historian. Hepworth's was in the Bull Ring opposite Old Meeting church very close to the river. Boots was on the north side of the High Street. Even if we allow that an alteration of the street level at these points is at all relevant to an alteration in Coventry Street, a change of four or five feet does not put the vault above street level. Instead, it suggests, as at Boots, the presence of an undercroft accessible from the street. This is exactly what McCave had seen in 1876. Kidderminster town centre is built on rising ground which slopes round in a curve. Therefore, it is likely that the base of some buildings, even if they were underground cellars for the most part, would take the form of an undercroft or basement emerging partially above ground in places. This, incidentally, is the most plausible explanation for any windows which have been observed in these cellars.

A close-up view of the mullioned window, interpreted by Hodgkins particularly as an "ecclesiastical" feature. The brick structure can clearly be seen, and it is thought that the mullions also were of brick. This was taken by Pycock and Wickett Ltd. of 2 Worcester Street probably in 1967. (BRO)

Hodgkins went on to raise three possibilities to substantiate the idea that the vault had been a chapel, all of which strain credulity. The first was a gild chapel. The Pope's register in 1401 had referred to such a Gild of the Holy Trinity in Kidderminster. The second option was a private chapel. Hodgkins noted that the arms of the Attwood family included the lion and the swan, and it was "at least a coincidence that near at hand they had the two inns, the Lion and the Swan." He posed the possibility that the family had a manor house nearby. He suggested they could see "nearby massive stones, of local sandstone, like those at Caldwall, which must have been part of a large building near the chapel." Unfortunately, there is no other known recorded reference to these stones and Hodgkins gives no information to help us identify them. The third suggestion, and for Hodgkins the "most likely", was that it was the chantry of St. Katherine, "believed hitherto to have been part of the Parish Church of St Mary's". In this instance Hodgkins was, as he acknowledged, going against the general opinion, and he did so without offering any evidence at all. It is known that this chantry was founded in 1469 by Lady Joyce Beauchamp, whose tomb is in the south aisle of St Mary's church, and to this day the best view is that the chantry was very close to it. Hodgkins bolsters his argument with the suggestion that Lady Beauchamp had a manor house close to the site of the vault. So both of these last two suggestions require us to believe that there was a manor house with grounds located across the Daddle Brook, on its Coventry Street side in the midst of the medieval town. There is no evidence for this at all.

Finally Hodgkins, perhaps recognising the flimsy nature of his theories, posed the possibility that if the chapel had always been underground after all, then the vault could have been "a refuge for the recusants of the reign of Queen Elizabeth."

I have been unable to locate an original photograph of A. J. Perrett. This picture of one of the town's most important and popular historians is reproduced from the centenary edition of the Shuttle, 13.2.1970.

It is noteworthy that the local authorities preferred to take advice elsewhere as they pursued their plans to demolish the vault which had excited Joe Perrett's interest for a quarter of a century. No public record of his opinion on the matter has come to light. He preferred to work quietly behind the scenes, and no doubt he gave his view to those who would listen.

A. J. Perrett's final Thoughts 1960

This latter theme was picked up, perhaps surprisingly, by the much respected local historian, Arthur Perrett, in 1960. He was a pupil of King Charles I Grammar School at Kidderminster, where he subsequently taught history for 39 years until his retirement in 1959. The twists and turns of his views at this late stage in his life show how difficult it was to reach any kind of certainty about the vault's origins even when it still existed to be closely observed. Perrett had sent an 18th century document to Harveys relating to their Kidderminster premises, and the local director, P. J. Lloyd, sent him a bottle of wine by way of thanks. This stimulated Perrett to quickly write an article on the history of the vaults, which he sent to Lloyd and which is contained in the Harveys archive. It was entitled "A Subterranean Chapel". In it Perrett dismissed McCave's theory that the vault was an early prison cell. Instead, he wrote of the Catholic Blount family living nearby in the manor house and of the legend that there was an underground passage from Harveys vaults to Hall Street and the church. He speculated that the Blount family, in an age of repression against Catholics, had required "a secret chapel where they could follow the faith of their choice". He referred to the discovery of the vault in 1851:

> "These contained human remains, and among other relics some curiously fashioned clay pipes. As tobacco smoking came to England in the latter years of Elizabeth's reign, the presence of the pipes helps to confirm a late Elizabethan origin of the chapel. It might well be that the human remains were those of Catholic priests who died there in hiding.... Until more discoveries come to light, it seems reasonable to

suppose then that the subterranean chapel in Swan Street is a relic of the days when religious persecution was rife, and that it was a concealed Catholic chapel."[12]

There are some weaknesses in this analysis, and the mysteries of the vaults were clearly continuing to elude the town's most respected historian. We must make allowances for the fact that he wrote this article quickly as a private letter. To begin with he was careless about the location of the vault, putting it in Swan Street when we know that it lay under 2 Coventry Street. Also, he glossed over the fact that the discovery in 1851 was of another vault lying well back from the main chapel-like vault. Another weakness running through this latest contribution is one he shared with all his predecessors, and that is that he assumed that the building was a chapel. In addition, he was prepared, without any basis whatsoever, to give credence to the idea that there was a secret passage. He stated: "There is a local tradition that an underground passage led from the Hall Street direction down towards where our underground chapel lies. Indeed, Church Street residents have avowed that such a passage exists."

On this occasion Perrett had completely rejected the question of a changing street level. He had abandoned the conclusion he had reached in 1935 when he then held the view that "it is now underground but was most likely on the street level when it was built."[13] Clearly, the vault could not have been both a secret hiding place for priests and located at street level. The uncertainty of Perrett is testimony in itself of the immense difficulty in solving the mystery of the vault's origins. However, his later view that, after all, it had always been "subterranean" is, I believe, the correct one.

Public Enquiry 1963

By 1963 the council had developed plans which required the demolition of Harveys and all neighbouring properties. At the public enquiry a brief description of the history of the cellars was offered, although no attempt was made to distinguish those under Harveys premises from the adjoining chapel-like vault which they leased. The county and borough councils had taken advice as to their architectural and historical merit and had decided they "were not worthy of preservation. There was no evidence that they had ever been other than domestic or used for the storage of beer and wine as they were now. The buildings over originally formed a timber-framed house dating from the late 16th or early 17th century. Cellars and original house were probably contemporary."[14]

The advice had been given in a report by Mr. Matley Moore. Significantly, the opinion of Kidderminster's own local historian, A. J. Perrett, does not seem to have been considered. Already by that time Perrett had clocked up over thirty years teaching of history at King Charles I school. By contrast, Moore was a dentist by profession and an interested amateur on historical questions. He was particularly interested in ecclesiastical buildings and was a member of the Worcester Diocesan Board. He had used his own money to restore his home The Greyfriars, in Friar Street. It is one of Worcestershire's finest timber-framed buildings. Clearly Moore was more interested in saving a late medieval building in Worcester than a merchant's cellar in Kidderminster. Kidderminster Borough Council seems to have sought an opinion which it knew would not stand in the way of its scheme. They would have known that Perrett had shown a belief in the historical importance of the cellars for several decades. There is an implicit snobbery in Moore's dismissal of merchants' cellars as having no historical merit. Just because they did not form part of an aristocratic house or ecclesiastical building, it does not follow that they were of little significance. On the contrary, had they survived they would have provided us with important historical evidence of the establishing of a town which one day was to attain international renown for its trade and industry. In addition, they would have given character to a town which now badly lacks it due to the depredations of the planners. It is ironic that we must agree with this assessment of the nature and dating of the cellars, but that is for the conclusion of this chapter.

Ian Walker 1968

A further collection of photographs appear to have been taken by Harveys prior to their departure from the premises. These were by Bernard A. Workman of 38 Comberton Park Road. These are useful, but by no means comprehensive. In fact, I cannot identify any pictures of the line of cellars under 1 Coventry Street. This was the first of a series of failures to engage in a successful recording exercise prior to the final destruction of the historic cellars. Even though by February 1968 the Inspector of Ancient Monuments had asked for some recording of the cellars before demolition, no record of any substance has been left.

The final contributor to this chapter is a local man, Ian Walker, who led a team from the town's Historical and Archaeological Society in some excavation during the last days. It was bad enough that the vaults were to be destroyed, but to add insult to injury the authorities failed to permit adequate time for a study of the structures which might have held a vital key to understanding Kidderminster's past. Ian Walker was clearly not properly prepared. He was caught between a government ministry which initially delayed his start because of doubts about his qualifications, before just letting him get on with it, and developers who hovered around with their bulldozer. Ian had not seen the vaults before, and he was surprised to find that the supposed chapel actually lay under no. 2 Coventry Street. He was surprised also by the lack of clear boundaries. On the downhill side he found that Harveys had "tunnelled through" to connect with the cellars next door in Swan Street. Unfortunately, this intriguing hint at the connection of cellars down the street is not followed up at all.

Frustratingly, Ian does not appear to have left any clear recording of what he discovered, which was supposed to be the object of the exercise. All that I have been able to discover is an unpublished article held at the library of Worcestershire's Historic Environment Record. It is clearly in draft form because right at the start there is an error in the date of his work, which he set at June 1964. These notes do not give sufficient detail to account for some of the conclusions. Ian discounted the legends that Harveys vaults led by underground passages both to St Mary's Church and to Caldwall Tower. Yet he gave no clear description of the termination of the warren of cellars he implied existed. In fact, there is no clear description of the network of cellars at all. The inadequacy of his work is further exposed in the light of the typed notes dated 3rd November 1967 by an unknown hand in the Harveys Bristol archive. These refer to the length of the cellars and "an underground passage which runs alongside the cellars to within an easy distance of the Church." Ian gave no substantial consideration to this possibility, even though Muriel Robinson's picture above and the photograph of a passage below strongly suggest that possible openings off the chapel-like vault did exist. Nor did he attempt to describe features which might have been the basis for the claims of previous historians that there was an altar or credence there. He was sceptical about the idea that the vault had been a chapel, but he dealt only with the small opening in the wall also containing the mullioned window and the Norman-style arched entrance. This "could have been interpreted as a leper squint. Presumably, it was the ecclesiastical style of this feature that must have given rise to the supposition that it was a chapel."

However, Ian did have time for some revealing observations. He formed the view that the vault "could not be earlier than Tudor, because it was built with bricks 8in x 4in x 2in of very good quality, no batts, chuffs or wasters were used." He described the spiral staircase, which they found behind a blocked up opening "on the right", which by implication of the rest of his notes was in the east wall of the putative chapel. It led up and curved back over the vault. He also noticed a wall made of bricks of 1901 from Chellingworth's Kidderminster brickworks which had "cut off the front end of the undercroft during the 1901 re-development."

Ian was very clear in his view that the vault was not a cellar, but had been an undercroft accessible from the street. He and his assistants had time to remove the brick floor and get down to an earlier brick floor which "showed where people had come down steps from the street and walked across it and through the "Norman" doorway." Although Ian did not mention it, this must have been the access from the street noted by McCave nearly a century before. Ian jumped extravagantly to the conclusion that Kidderminster had a two-decker shopping centre similar to the Rows in Chester, but he provided no additional evidence for this. We might rest with his sound observation and opinion in the unpublished article that the cellar was once an undercroft for commercial use. Unfortunately, more doubt as to Ian's final view was raised when it was reported in July 1968 that "in view of the nature of some of the window openings, Mr Walker feels it more likely that the building was at some time used for religious purposes than that it was not."[15]

Conclusion

After the struggle of earlier historians, modern archaeological methods might well have been able to date the vault and clarify its original purpose had it survived. Unfortunately, the philistine local council of the 1960s, unable to show the same concern for the town's history as their predecessors of the late 19th century, destroyed these wine cellars forever. Therefore, the conclusions reached by this book are inevitably qualified by doubt. This will remain the case unless there is an unexpected discovery of old documents, such as Meredith's detailed plan. The best view is that the vault was built by a wealthy merchant in the late 16th century or early 17th century. In it he stored his valuable commodities, which may well have included cloth, before it was transported away from Kidderminster, and wine unloaded at Bewdley after being conveyed up the Severn. The identity of that merchant remains unknown, and considerable study will be required to reveal him.

The above photograph was taken by Fortens c1957. The passageway shown is the same as in the photograph on the right. It is running away from the north end of the vault towards New Meeting. The slope of the roof indicates that this passage must be on the north side of the vault opposite the wall with the arched doorway and the mullioned window facing Coventry Street. So this is not the bricked up passageway on the east side mentioned by Ian Walker. (BRO)

On the left is one of a number of photographs taken by Workman in 1967 before demolition. (Muriel Robinson's picture shown earlier in the chapter may show this opening.) Someone has typed a note on the back of this picture: "This bricked-up passageway leading from the crypt may conceal historical secrets which the demolition teams will strip bare in the new year." Unhappily, demolition proceeded with no record taken of this passageway and what lay beyond it. (BRO)

Footnotes

[1] Professor Blair's comments are contained in an email sent to Victoria. His guess was that the traceried window was "rather crude 14th century" and that the vault itself " also looks 14th – 15th century".

[2] A copy of the article is in the library of the Historic Environment Record.

[3] I am grateful to Wyre Forest District Council for access to their collection of deeds held in their legal department. The poor rate list for 1790 is held at Kidderminster Library. That for 1798 is at WRO ref: BA10470/170.

[4] Worcestershire Chronicle 15.5.1851.

[5] See p15 of a volume of Guest's articles entitled "Old Kidderminster" in Kidderminster Library

[6] I am grateful to Bob Millward for providing me with extracts from his transcription of the diary.

[7] McCave's work is bound in a volume held at Kidderminster library. The relevant articles are dated 13.5.1876 and 15.7.1876.

[8] This is from the deeds held by Wyre Forest District Council. I have been unable to find in the council minutes or newspaper reports any explicit reason for treating the Fleece differently, so the need for conservation of the historic cellar must be presumed to have been uppermost in the minds of councillors.

[9] For Perrett's talk see KS 4.5.1935. For Hodgkin's visit see KS 31.8.1935.

[10] T.R.Nash, Collections for the History of Worcestershire (1782), p37.

[11] The proposed deed of gift by Watson is among the deeds held by Wyre Forest District Council. Guest's observations are in his seventh 1905 article, see KS 6.5.1905. For the savings bank reference, see Burton, op. cit., p48. Perrett's view on the location of the manor house is in his private 1960 article discussed later in this chapter.

[12] BRO ref: 40913/Ph/4/7

[13] This is contained in a series of articles Perrett produced called "Do you know?" See KS 24.8.1935.

[14] For public enquiry, see KS 6.12.1963. The source of the historical advice was not disclosed by this report, but Moore's name was later revealed by the Kidderminster Times 2.2.1968.

[15] Worcestershire Archaeology Newsletter No. 2 July 1968 held at HER.

Chapter Nine

The final Years

Despite the shock of her husband's death, Lydia Harvey took control of the Kidderminster business. Her period in charge was to run for over twelve years, before she too died unexpectedly. The evidence suggests that she carried out her task competently, despite a lack of confidence in her at Bristol. Having toyed with the idea of selling it for many years, head office probably had little interest in the small subsidiary for a while. However, a profit continued to be made, and it may be that after the war, under the chairmanship of Jack Harvey until 1956, the Bristol board of directors was more supportive.

Letters of 1943 and 1944 show that the parent company was then actively looking at disposing of the Kidderminster business. The first letter is the one dated 1st December 1943, which was mentioned above, disclosing the old opinion of Edward Harvey that Kidderminster should be closed down. It has survived as a typed copy, and it was evidently written by one of the directors, almost certainly Bertie Wright, who had for some years been Edward's trusted lieutenant. He had been added to the list of directors of the Kidderminster branch in 1939. During the war much of the burden of running the Bristol business fell on his shoulders whilst John Harvey IV, known as "Jack", was away in Wales working for MI5. Jack had no record of hostility to Kidderminster after he took over as chairman in 1937, but during the war years the retired chairman, Eddie Harvey, was probably free to influence Wright. The tone was patronising towards Lydia Harvey. The writer referred to an audit by their accountant, George Goode of Impey Cudworth & Co., which had revealed "an unhealthy state of affairs" at Charles Harvey & Co., and expressed sorrow that Lydia "did not tell us how things were and ask for some advice". It was admitted, somewhat paradoxically, that "since the war started the business has, of course, been much more prosperous on paper but the unfortunate position is that all the extra profit made has been of no benefit to us as principal shareholders as it has had to be paid away in E.P.T."

E.P.T., or Excess Profits Tax, was introduced in World War Two. Pre-war profit levels of companies were treated no differently in wartime, but additional taxation was levied on increased profits in order to prevent profiteering and to fund the war effort. This was at first set at 60% and soon increased to 100%, but with 20% to be repaid as deferred credit at the end of the war. This was, of course, not Lydia's fault, but the tone of the letter seemed to suggest she should have found a way to put some extra profit in the way of the shareholders.

The writer went on to say that "stock has been disposed of which we cannot replace." The company was worried that the wine trade would continue in a poor state after the war. They were thinking of selling the Kidderminster business to a firm of brewers. No wine merchant would be interested because "you have so little stock to offer". The letter's final words at last came to the point that Kidderminster was to be sacrificed to give the holding company a post-war boost. "The position is just this, that we have a fair amount of capital locked up in C. H. & Co. which we could use to better advantage here when rebuilding and restocking has to be faced, and we want to take advantage of the present situation if possible."

The writer was anxious to reassure Lydia concerning her own personal position. "I know you will be worrying about your own position, but I would like to ease your mind on this point and assure you that we should look after you in generous fashion, as we have no intention of making things difficult for you... For the moment please don't worry and let things rest as they are until we meet." Lydia had no children, and although she had been working as director at Charles Harvey & Co. only since 1940, she had probably helped her husband run the business since they arrived in Kidderminster in 1922. Yet it did not seem to occur to her correspondent that she might wish to carry on working.

The second letter was dated September 1944 and was written by the accountant, George Goode, to Jack Harvey, the chairman of the Bristol company and thereby of the Kidderminster subsidiary. This made it quite clear that the accountant was against the idea of selling, and the initiative must have been coming from the Bristol Board of Directors. Goode's view was, of course, based on a hard-nosed look at the figures. He valued the assets at a little over £15,500. This included £5000 for the property, £3700 for stocks, and £200 for the fleet of motor vehicles, which amounted to just one car and two vans. The preference shareholders would have to be paid £7,500. There would be insufficient to provide Lydia with a pension or to make the deal attractive to ordinary shareholders. Regarding the latter group's stake of £7500, Goode estimated they would get less than the £1 value of each share, probably in fact less than 17 shillings.

Goode ended optimistically. He pointed out that, far from being unprofitable, Charles Harvey & Co. "is at present paying 10% dividend on ordinary shares, and is gradually improving its reserves." He advised Jack Harvey to persevere with Kidderminster, adding "if after the war you can get a keen manager for £600 - £700 plus a bonus on results, there is no reason why C. H. & Co. should not continue to earn satisfactory profits." Again, it did not seem to occur to them that the management already in place might be fully able to run the business. But Kidderminster was reprieved, and in fact Lydia was left to carry on running things.

Some sales records survive for the years 1945 to 1949. These suggest that, under Lydia's management, sales increased until her sudden death. During the last months of the war, sales seem to have amounted to a little over £3000 per month. There was slow growth for a few months, before rising to well over £4000 per month and sometimes over £5000 until at least February 1948. So, for example, sales for the year beginning 1st March 1947 increased by £11,367 over the previous year, well above the rate of inflation which was then at about 7.7%. There was a tailing off afterwards, and sales for the period from 1st March 1948 increased only by a figure which could be accounted for by inflation. "Some dividend" was declared for the company's shareholders in 1950.[1] It has been written more recently that "the Kidderminster business was operating at a loss shortly after the Second World War and was wound down".[2] The truth is probably that Charles Harvey & Co. Ltd was profitable, but not sufficiently so to form part of the expanding holding company's long term plans.

Lydia died on Christmas Day 1950 after a short illness, whilst still the managing director of Charles Harvey & Co. Ltd. After living at Elmhurst, Blakedown, for a time during the war years, she finished her life living on her own at Flat 2 of Springfield House, being number 71

Stourbridge Road in Kidderminster. Important members of the Harvey family from Bristol were present at the funeral at St. Ambrose's Catholic Church. These included John Harvey, the chairman, and George McWatters with his wife. McWatters was the grandson of Edward Harvey, who had been chairman of the Bristol company until his death in 1910, and was to become chairman himself in 1956.[3]

Post-war shortage and Bristol blending

The Bristol company also struggled after the war. Sales conferences reported shortages of Bristol Milk and Bristol Cream, which were to ease only by early 1954. At their sales conference in February 1951 George McWatters interestingly revealed that their "large exports to dollar countries" had priority over shipments to this country, which clearly showed the importance of the American market to Harveys. He went on to refer to a fundamental change they were introducing in the production process of sherry. He said:

> *"The shortage is being overcome by recent purchases of further old wine in Spain, which we were extremely fortunate to obtain. This will require time to blend. The blending of Bristol Milk and Bristol Cream will in future take place in Bristol, and, though we do not wish to offer this information to all comers, it is a useful answer to those who accuse us of merely purchasing other shippers' wines."*[4]

This draws attention to the fact that Harveys Bristol Cream, famous throughout the world, had always been blended for them by Spanish wine producers. The name 'Bristol Cream' was legally Harveys, and nobody else could use the brand. Yet all the company had done was to bottle it when it arrived at Bristol. This was a historic change, but only for a short period. Certainly by the end of the decade Harveys were again importing sherry already blended.

Mr. E. R. Warder, Kidderminster

Edwin Warder. "Dick", as he was known, was manager of the branch for around thirty years until c1957. (BRO)

There was no longer a member of the Harvey family to run the Kidderminster branch, and Mr M. W. R. Pease was appointed Managing Director from 1st April 1951 at a salary of £1500.[5] Still in post as manager of the branch was the long-serving Dick Warder, who attended the six-monthly sales conferences held by the parent company during this period. It is clear that Kidderminster held responsibility for managing sales in part of the Midlands, including Worcestershire and Warwickshire. After Mrs Harvey's death, this responsibility had to be temporarily transferred until Mr Pease took over. For a time it seems that Kidderminster was holding its own. Mr Pease reported good progress at the regular sales conferences until at least 1953. His Bristol bosses were evidently pleased with him, because from 1st March 1956 he left to take up position in Manchester as director and vice-chairman of a new subsidiary R. W. Hilton & Co. Ltd. at a salary of £2250 plus entertaining allowance of £150.

It may be that some sort of watershed was reached for Kidderminster at this time. The parent company was expanding. For some years it had been developing the American market. The chairman, Jack Harvey, had spent much of his time in the United States in the early 1950s after George McWatters joined the Bristol Board in 1949 as Home Sales Director.[6] His work was very successful, and later, as shown in the company's 1962 annual report, the United States and Canada had become Harveys' most important export markets. Kidderminster had no substantial place any longer in this international company. Its declining importance was reflected in the salary given to Pease's replacement as managing director, Mr. J. H. Boys. He received £1350 plus £150 entertaining allowance from 1st March 1956, which was considerably less than Pease's salary when he had started in 1951.[7]

Mr. L. Bachelor, Kidderminster

Mr. J. H. Boys, Managing Director at Kidderminster

Two popular figures at Harveys in the 1950s. "Batch", the cellar foreman, had completed 44 years with the company by 1957. One of his tasks was the decanting of the finest port. John Harvey Boys arrived at Kidderminster in 1956, and his departure c1960 was probably the beginning of the end for the branch. (BRO)

Shortages at Kidderminster – "Port and Sherry"

The year 1956 saw Harveys of Bristol record their highest ever turnover at £2½m. Yet they were unable to guarantee their Kidderminster subsidiary the supplies they needed. At a sales conference in April of that year, Dick Warder reported hold-ups in supplies from Bristol and asked if provisional reserves could be held for them in Bristol. This request was denied on the grounds of a shortage of space at Head Office.

John Harvey V tells an amusing story of how an unusual drink caught on in Kidderminster. At some point during the shortages a pub, having received the necessary deliveries, put a sign outside advertising port and sherry at sixpence. Customers started to come in asking for a glass of "port and sherry". This carried on until years later John was standing at a bar in the town and was startled to hear a woman order a glass of this strange concoction. He informed her amiably that he had never heard of such a drink, but of course she had no idea of his identity.

Charles Harvey, son of James, and the forgotten man of the family, died in March 1957 at the age of 85. His death was another stage towards the impending removal of the Harvey name from Kidderminster business life. After the closure in 1927 of his vacuum cleaner factory nothing is known of any further work done by Charles. The funeral took place at St. John's Church on 4th March. Unlike previous Harvey funerals, no significant family members from Bristol were in attendance. The mourners included three daughters Joan, Rachel and Diana Harvey. Also present were Mr and Mrs H. S. Poole, being his other daughter, Ruth, and her husband. The short obituary shed no light on the deceased's career.[8]

At around the same time, in February 1957, head office's finance committee reported disappointment with sales figures for Kidderminster, but this was put down to the slowness with which invoices were being sent to Bristol.[9] Possibly the Kidderminster office was going through a period of adjustment. In addition to the appointment of a new managing director, there had been a major change with the retirement of Dick Warder as manager of the branch, probably in 1956, after three decades with the company. He was replaced by another local man, Bob Poyner. According to Mary Lawson, who worked at Harveys as a young woman for a few years from 1958, the new management team was popular with the staff. John Boys had worked at the Portsmouth branch of Harveys for six years before coming to Kidderminster as managing director. It seems as if there was no intention to wind down the operation at that stage. Indeed, new offices were built at the rear of the Swan Street premises in 1957. But events were unfolding to make the future of the Kidderminster branch very uncertain.

The rapid growth of the holding company in Bristol saw the accelerated demise of its traditional concentration on the direct supply of private customers. When the young Mary Lawson joined Charles Harvey & Co. in the late 1950s, she became immediately aware that the tradition of dealing with the aristocracy and gentry was alive and well in Kidderminster. During her early duties on the switchboard she received a call from Lord Sandys of Ombersley, who required a bottle of his seriously expensive port, which he referred to by its bin number as his '1001'. Understandably confusing this with a well-known cleaning product, Mary advised him to try Timothy White's. This faux pas produced a bit of a dressing-down from her boss, but Lord Sandys was very kind and later told her that the incident had caused much laughter at many dinner parties. Yet it was already clear at the April 1958 sales conference that the change to supplying wholesalers was well in hand. In 1960 it was reported that supplying the requirements of personal customers directly was still "cherished" by the company, but the supply of the trade and wholesalers had grown enormously, embracing hotels, breweries and mail order houses. Later still, a three-year plan drawn up by the Bristol company for the period from April 1964 saw the creation of a force of senior men to handle selling to wholesalers. The report described the development of such sales as of the "greatest importance".[10]

Launch as a public company

John Harvey & Sons Ltd. of Bristol remained a private limited company, but the need for further expansion pointed towards launching themselves as a public company. As part of the preparations for this move, the parent company decided to convert the subsidiaries into direct branches administratively, but postponed the actual liquidation of these companies. The name of the Manchester subsidiary was changed to John Harvey (Manchester) Ltd and by January 1958 it was being converted to branch administration. Similarly Cardiff and Kidderminster became branches on 1st September 1958 pending liquidation. Charles Harvey & Co. Ltd. became Charles Harvey & Co., Midlands Branch of John Harvey & Sons Ltd., Bristol.

With the subsidiaries now brought under their complete control, the Bristol board moved towards conversion into a public company. The decision to proceed was agreed by an Extraordinary General Meeting of the private company's shareholders on 12th November 1958. So successful was the subsequent share issue that two years later The Times described this conversion as "one of the most outstanding of its time". There were 80,000 applications for over 46 million five shilling shares, when only 800,000 were available. The 400,000 £1 preference shares attracted 5,300 applications for nearly 3 million shares.

The ambitious expansion of the company meant that inefficient sectors could no longer be tolerated. The massively increased volume of trade being handled by Harveys required modern facilities. A huge new storage depot at Whitchurch on the south side of Bristol epitomised the new age. It was a state of the art warehouse and bottling plant opened in October 1960 by the President of the Board of Trade, Reginald Maudling. The sherry arrived correctly blended from the soleras of the company's organisation in Jerez. It was at first stored, but after a short time it was transferred to huge glass-lined bottling tanks. There were ten tanks each having a capacity of 5,500 gallons and twenty tanks with a capacity of 2,200 gallons.

In addition other new depots across the country were created. By late 1959, for example, a site had been purchased at Rubery on the edge of Birmingham, and soon new premises were built which provided speedy despatch via the motorway network. The writing was very much on the wall for the Kidderminster branch. Around 1960 John Boys moved on and was replaced by a Mr Sanders. It was evident to the staff that Sanders' job was to wind down the branch. Staff members were taken over to view the Rubery premises, and it was made clear to them that they could secure their future by moving there. Very few took up this offer. The Rubery base was to become Harvey's Midlands Sales Office. Kidderminster with its ancient cellars and its distance from the motorway was no longer relevant to Harveys distribution process.

By 1963 the final threat to its future was well advanced. The borough council was busy with plans to build a ring road and to demolish much of the historic town centre. These included a scheme for a new shopping complex which was to be called the Swan Centre, and required the demolition of the whole of Swan Street and part of Coventry Street, including Harveys. There was opposition from some of the businesses affected, which was revealed at the public enquiry into the plan. Harveys led a move to form a consortium of freeholders to develop a counter-proposal. One of the directors, J. N. Mostyn, admitted that the Kidderminster premises were "dilapidated", but it was the firm's policy "to retain their freeholds and to develop and improve them wherever possible."[11] Nothing came of this.

Two glimpses of the modern premises at Rubery, south-west of Birmingham and close to the motorway network. These facilities made Kidderminster's cellars obsolete. (BRO)

Takeover

If there was any possibility that the company might still want to fight for the retention of the Kidderminster site, which held so many memories for the Harvey family, then these were finally quashed by a takeover beginning in 1965. The last vestiges of a fine family company were rapidly disappearing, as Harveys was swallowed up by a larger company and began its transformation into part of a rootless international conglomerate. Harveys was probably ripe for a takeover. The Sunday Times observed that "not only have earnings per ordinary share remained practically static since going public in 1958 but it is virtually a one-product company: 75% of the profits come from the best selling Bristol Cream."[12] The successful bid was by Showerings, which had made a fortune with its Babycham product. At that time its annual profits were £5.5m as compared with those of Harveys at £1.12m.[13]

Harveys initially resisted the takeover by Showerings, and preferred a rival bid by Beechams, the drug company. In August 1965 Showerings made a bid worth 21s 1d for each share in Harveys. This was rejected rather strongly, with the board of Harveys indicating that a bid of 25s might be acceptable. Showerings withdrew and in early December a bid by Beechams was received close to this valuation. The chairman, George McWatters, indicated that he and his co-directors and their families were inclined to accept it for their 30% holding of ordinary shares. It is interesting that they preferred a bid by a company making pills, soft drinks and haircream to one by a company already making and selling wines as well as cider and Babycham. The reason may well have been Beechams' strength in marketing in the United States. Harveys were doing well there and Bristol Cream had been an extraordinary success. Yet there was still huge untapped potential for growth in a country where disposable income had risen fast since 1951. It had been noted by The Times in 1960 that Harveys sherry sales in the Unites States had remained almost static in that period.

In the end, however, a further bid of £12.8m by Showerings in December 1965 was impossible to resist. The complex offer involved one share plus £2 5s worth of 7¼% convertible stock plus 9s 6d cash for every three Harveys shares. Those who did not want the swap could sell their ordinary shares for 23s 6d cash.[14] The Sunday Times reported that the Harveys family were 'swallowing their pride' and McWatters 'ran up the white flag'. The Board of Directors wrote to the shareholders advising them to accept an offer valued at around 26s a share.

Closure

For the next two years Harveys continued in business in Kidderminster until the inevitable end. On 30th December 1967 the doors were finally closed. It was a time when there was little interest in heritage, and progress and prosperity seemed to beckon Kidderminster with its flourishing carpet industry. There was no obvious opposition from the public to the plans. Nevertheless, there was a brief scare for the planners in January 1968 when the Chief Inspector of Ancient Monuments questioned whether Harveys' cellars should be preserved after all. Fearing the abandonment of the Swan Centre scheme by the developers, Hammersons, the borough Town Clerk, John Evans, simply drew the Inspector's attention to the report of Matley Moore, and the Inspector withdrew his objections. The Worcester dentist had been given the last word.[15]

However, the Inspector did insist on one condition, that the "Royal Commission on Historical Monuments were given opportunity to carry out recording operations before their demolition". Kidderminster Historical and Archaeological Society tried to make the best of the situation. A group lead by Ian Walker bravely attempted some excavation, as outlined in the previous chapter. Demolition was already underway when he began his work. In fact, the demolition contractor threatened Walker at one point that he would "drop a chimney across us if we didn't go away." Finally, the investigation was terminated by the abrupt intervention of the bulldozer. The complete failure of the authorities to ensure that the Inspector's modest ruling was given effect means that today we have no detailed record of the cellars and vaults. Therefore, the conclusions reached by this book, it has to be admitted, lack certainty.

This picture is a late one, probably from 1967.
The false gables which concealed a flat roof have been removed. (BRO)

Within days of the closure of the branch, an article in The Times illustrated the fast-changing world which no longer required its services. Cut-price competition in the £650m wine and spirits market was alarming small wine merchants. Retail licences were being granted to growing numbers of supermarkets. The chairman of Tesco said that his stores provided drink sales to customers who preferred one-stop shopping. "The wine habit is catching on in this country, and people want to buy their wine and spirits at the same time as they buy their food." The marketing director of Bass-Charrington Vintners, the wine and spirits subsidiary of Britain's biggest brewery group added: "A supermarket could never offer the range carried by an off licence. The wine habit is growing so fast that there is room for everybody."[16]

Unfortunately, as far as making room is concerned, there is little sentiment in modern capitalism. After the demise of the Kidderminster branch, there was ultimately to be little place at all in Britain for Harveys wine merchants, which gradually disappeared within an ever-expanding group. Showerings and their associated businesses, including Harveys, were merged with Allied Breweries in 1968. A drift towards relocation in Spain began in 1970 with the purchase of the sherry producer, Mackenzie & Co., which had been one of their suppliers. The group became Allied Lyons in 1978 after the purchase of J. Lyons & Co. By 1989 the production and distribution of Harveys sherry was carried out completely from Spain, after Harveys left their bottling plant in south Bristol, built only thirty years previously. Thus European regulations requiring bottling in the country of origin were satisfied. In 1994 Allied Lyons merged with Pedro Domecq to form Allied Domecq.[17] In 2003 the Bristol offices in Denmark Street finally closed down, and to all intents and purposes the real historic Harveys had ceased to exist, although for a few years a distribution base at Horsham still used the name John Harvey & Sons. In 2005 Pernod Ricard took over Allied Domecq, and soon afterwards an American company, Fortune Brands, purchased over 25 of its wine and spirit brands. These included the fine Harveys sherries. In July 2009 the remaining staff and stock of the English business still carrying the Harvey name were purchased by the Lincolnshire firm of Walker and Wodehouse, who now distribute the wines and hold the Royal Warrant. The Harvey name lives on, but only as a brand. As a company name, it has been filed away.[18]

Footnotes

[1] This was at the Directors Meeting 28.4.1950 - BRO ref: 40913/M/1/1.
[2] Catalogue of the Records of Harveys of Bristol, p2.
[3] KS 29.12.1950.
[4] BRO ref: 40913/M/1/1.
[5] This was reported at the directors meeting on 3rd January 1951. The salary, unsurprisingly, was a moderate one and would be worth about £35,000 in 2010.
[6] Sunday Telegraph 31.1.1993.
[7] The salary Pease started with in 1951 would have been worth about £1800 in 1956.
[8] KS 8.3.1957.
[9] BRO ref: 40913/M/2/1.
[10] See The Times 3.10.1960 and BRO ref: 40913/R/1/3.
[11] KS 6.12.1963.
[12] Sunday Times 19.12.1965.
[13] Birmingham Post 14.12.1965.
[14] Daily Mail 14.12.1965.
[15] Kidderminster Times 2.2.1968.
[16] The Times 4.1.1968.
[17] The house of Domecq went back to the early nineteenth century in Jerez, where their vineyards had been established by 1730 by an Irish wine grower, Patrick Murphy.
[18] I thank John Harvey V and Robin Wodehouse for explaining this to me.

Sources Used

Abbreviations used in this book

BRO   Bristol Record Office   KL   Kidderminster Library
WRO Worcester Record Office   KS   Kidderminster Shuttle

Primary Sources

The Harveys archive held at BRO, ref: 40913. Also at BRO, two recently discovered boxes containing the Kidderminster records, which are not yet part of the classified collection. (It is possible these might be transferred to Worcester Record Office in due course.)

Deeds held by Wyre Forest District Council. There is no open access to this collection, but between 2006 and 2008 I was able to view them on behalf of the Historic Kidderminster project. They include those for 3-7 Coventry St and the Clarence Inn, which have been used for this book. Some of the older deeds may be transferred to WRO.

Minutes of Town Council held at KL.

Bills of Entry held at Bristol Central Library and Liverpool Maritime Museum give details of wine imported into the two ports.

Photographs

Many of the photographs used are from BRO. Some of them are contained in the two unclassified boxes mentioned above. Others are in the main Harvey collection. These include a bundle of photos, many being of the cellars, ref: 40913/Ph/4/7. The photograph of the Board of Directors from 1937 is ref: 40913/Ph/1/8. Those of the Rubery premises are ref: 40913/Ph/4/1. The three photographs of staff members at Kidderminster in the final chapter are from the company magazine, The Cellarman, in 1957 ref: 40913/St/4/1.

Articles etc

"The Excavation of Harvey's Vault and Discovery of a surprising Piece of Kidderminster's Medieval History", by Charles Ian Walker F.S.A. (unpublished - copy held at Historic Environment Record in Worcester)

Journal/Diary between 8th January 1856 and 2nd August 1857 of George Edward Roberts 1831-65, transcribed by Bob Millward (2010)

"Harveys of Bristol, wine merchants: some aspects of its past with particular reference to the period 1829-1839" by Robert Sterling (1971). A university dissertation held at BRO ref: 40913/H/1/15

Books (most recent first)

St. George's: A Waterloo Church, Melvyn Thompson (2010)
Bristol's Floating Harbour, Peter Malpass and Andy King (2009)
Catalogue of the Records of Harveys of Bristol, Bristol Record Office (2004)
A History of Kidderminster, Nigel Gilbert (2004)
For Valour: Kidderminster's Four V.C.s, Ruth Butler and Don Gilbert (2000)
Severn Traders, Colin Green (1999)
Tales of the River Severn, Chris Witts (1998)
Lots of Bottle, Helen Reid (1996)
The Oxford illustrated History of Roman Britain, Peter Salway (1993)
Sherry, Julian Jeffs. (1992)
The Widening Gate: Bristol and the Atlantic Economy 1450-1700, David Harris Sacks (1991)
Bewdley in its Golden Age, Bewdley Historical Research Group (1991)
The City of Worcester in the Sixteenth Century, Alan D. Dyer (1973)
Bristol Cream, Godfrey Harrison (1955)
The Severn Valley, John Randall (1862)
Collections for the History of Worcestershire, T.R. Nash (1782)

In January 2008 this plaque was erected by the Civic Society at the entrance to the Swan Centre and unveiled by John Harvey V. The research undertaken since then for this book has switched the balance of the evidence in favour of a merchant's cellar with a date slightly later than the medieval period.

Harvey/Jotham Family Network

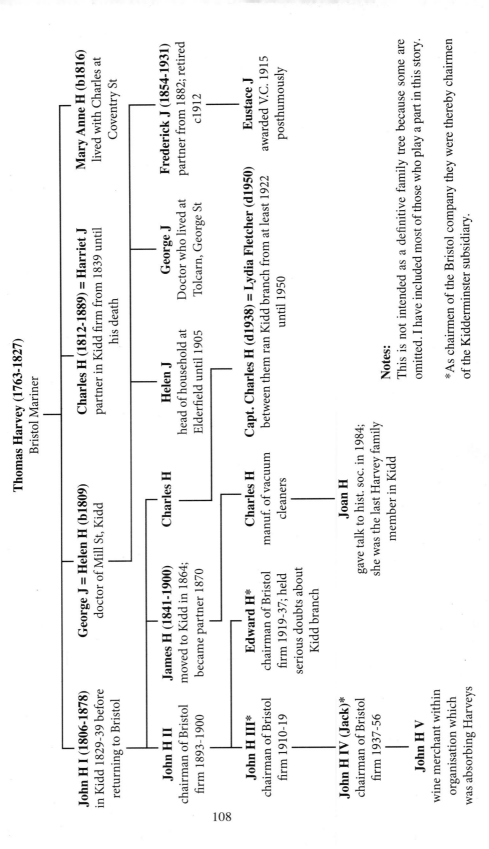

Thomas Harvey (1763-1827)
Bristol Mariner

Charles H (1812-1889) = Harriet J
partner in Kidd firm from 1839 until
his death

Mary Anne H (b1816)
lived with Charles at
Coventry St

George J = Helen H (b1809)
doctor of Mill St, Kidd

George J
Doctor who lived at
Tolcarn, George St

Frederick J (1854-1931)
partner from 1882; retired
c1912

John H I (1806-1878)
in Kidd 1829-39 before
returning to Bristol

Charles H

Helen J
head of household at
Elderfield until 1905

Capt. Charles H (d1938) = Lydia Fletcher (d1950)
between them ran Kidd branch from at least 1922
until 1950

Eustace J
awarded V.C. 1915
posthumously

John H II
chairman of Bristol
firm 1893-1900

James H (1841-1900)
moved to Kidd in 1864;
became partner 1870

Charles H
manuf. of vacuum
cleaners

Joan H
gave talk to hist. soc. in 1984;
she was the last Harvey family
member in Kidd

John H III*
chairman of Bristol
firm 1910-19

Edward H*
chairman of Bristol
firm 1919-37; held
serious doubts about
Kidd branch

John H IV (Jack)*
chairman of Bristol
firm 1937-56

John H V
wine merchant within
organisation which
was absorbing Harveys

Notes:
This is not intended as a definitive family tree because some are
omitted. I have included most of those who play a part in this story.

* As chairmen of the Bristol company they were thereby chairmen
of the Kidderminster subsidiary.